# Miller's Waves

## An Informal Scientific Biography

**William Fickinger**

Department of Physics
Case Western Reserve University
Cleveland, Ohio 44106

| Library of Congress Control Number: | | 2011903312 |
|---|---|---|
| ISBN: | Hardcover | 978-1-4568-7746-0 |
| | Softcover | 978-1-4568-7745-3 |
| | Ebook | 978-1-4568-7747-7 |



This book was printed in the United States of America.

**To order additional copies of this book, contact:**
Xlibris Corporation
1-888-795-4274
www.Xlibris.com
Orders@Xlibris.com
93810

# Contents

# Preface

Dayton C. Miller was an American physicist who, in the early decades of the twentieth century, was well-known for his scientific research and for his ability to convey its meaning to the public. He was the chairman of the Physics Department at the Case School of Applied Science in Cleveland from 1893 until 1938. This informal biography is the first effort to present a complete chronological description of all of Miller's research. He was interested in a variety of experimental physics topics, and much has been published about different aspects of his work. For example, his pioneering experiments in the early use of x-rays have been described in the medical history literature. His work on the analysis of musical and spoken sounds is described in the acoustics literature. Miller's unique collection of flutes and related materials, today maintained by the Library of Congress, is well-known in the world of musicology.

Most recent writing about Miller concerns his determined efforts unambiguously to detect the luminiferous ether—the substance that was presumed to fill all of space and which supports the passage of light. This had been a major challenge to experimental physicists for several decades, from the time of the 1887 Michelson-Morley experiment until well after the arrival on the physics scene of Einstein's relativity theory. Miller was a well-known and respected member of the American physics community and, because he had earlier worked on the ether search with Morley, it seemed a natural venture for him to pursue. For at least a decade, he was encouraged by many in the physics community in his efforts to discover why Michelson and Morley had failed to find clear evidence for the ether. Miller's work in the 1920s at the Mt. Wilson Observatory in California was of great interest to the world physics community, which was split between those seeking the verification of the “classical” ether theory and those who placed their bets on Einstein’s remarkable and, for many, counter-intuitive, relativity theory. Miller thus found himself at the center of a world-wide decade-long debate concerning the validity of relativity.

# Acknowledgments

I am grateful to the following people who have helped me put together this story of Dayton Miller's physics career: Helen Conger and Jill Tatum of the Case Western Reserve University Archives; Sue Hanson of the Kelvin Smith Special Collections at CWRU; John Grabowski of the Western Reserve Historical Society; Louise Kiefer of the Baldwin Wallace University Archives; Peter Hoekje of Baldwin Wallace University; David Pantalony of the Canada Science and Technology Museum; and Carol Lynn Ward Bamford, archivist of the Dayton C. Miller Flute Collection at the Library of Congress. Many details of Miller's life and research are found in his personal files, which were so carefully preserved in the CWRU Physics Department Archives by the late Robert S. Shankland and Arthur H. Benade.

I thank my colleagues at Case Western Reserve University who read and commented on the text: David E. Farrell, Kenneth L. Kowalski, Philip L. Taylor, D. Keith Robinson, Peter Pesch, Alan Rocke, and James Edmonson. Special thanks go to physics historian Professor Thomas Greenslade of Kenyon College. I enjoyed informative conversations about Miller with Marcelo Teo of the University of Sao Paulo and with Roberto Lalli of the University of Milan, each of whom is, in 2011, completing a doctoral dissertation related to Dayton Miller's research.

William Fickinger<br>
Cleveland, Ohio

# Chapter 1 Youth

The town of Strongsville is about twelve miles southwest of Cleveland in that northeast corner of Ohio once known as the Western Reserve of the State of Connecticut. The Reserve is a strip of land stretching a hundred miles along the southern shore of Lake Erie. Historically, it was a small section of a ribbon of land reaching due west from Connecticut all the way to the Pacific. It was granted to the Connecticut colony by King Charles II in the 1660s. After sorting out competing claims by the states of New York and Pennsylvania, and by resident Indian tribes, Connecticut established ownership in 1785 of three million acres. About a sixth of this was reserved for settlers from New England who suffered losses in the Revolutionary war. The rest was sold to land developers who, in 1796, sent Moses Cleaveland and a team of surveyors to map it out in preparation for its development. Only seven years later, Ohio became the seventeenth state, with the city of Cleveland at the center of its Lake Erie coastline.

Early settlers from New England made their way westward across New York state by wagon, and, after 1824, by barge on the newly opened Erie Canal, which ran from the Hudson River to Lake Erie. Then in 1832, the Ohio and Erie Canal began north-south operation connecting Cleveland and the Ohio River. This established the city as a significant transportation hub, attracting an influx of new settlers and new commerce. In the 1840s, dozens of small inter-city steam railroad lines came into service. That network of independent lines was soon woven into a passenger and freight rail system which, by the late 1850s, connected Cleveland with New York, Pittsburgh, Cincinnati, and Chicago. Especially important for the rapid growth of the Cleveland area was railroad access to coal from Pennsylvania and lake-steamer access to Minnesota for iron ore to feed its burgeoning steel mills.

Following the earlier settlers from the eastern states who were mostly farmers, large numbers of immigrants, including refugees from the Irish potato famine, arrived in the Cleveland area in the 1830s and '40s. There they found work in its mills and factories. By 1870, the surrounding Cuyahoga County population had reached one hundred thirty thousand. In only seven decades, the Western Reserve developed from what was essentially Indian territory, visited occasionally by French fur traders, to a bustling manufacturing and transportation center.

Among the New England settlers who made their way to Strongsville was seventeen-year-old Alanson Pomeroy. He arrived there from Massachusetts with his parents in 1822. Nine years later, Alanson married, and he and his wife Keziah eventually raised nine children. Mr. Pomeroy became a leading citizen, businessman, and justice of the peace. He was the founder and director of the bank in the nearby town of Berea. In the difficult years of the Civil War, the Pomeroy family played a significant role in the Underground Railway, helping runaway slaves reach the shores of Lake Erie, where they might find passage to Canada. In 1863, Vienna Pomeroy, one of Alanson's daughters, married a young fellow named Charles Miller. Twenty-two-year-old Miller, son of another settler from New England, was born in Ravenna, a town about thirty miles southeast of Cleveland.

Charles and Vienna's firstborn child is the subject of our story. Dayton Clarence Miller was born on 13 March in 1866 in the elegant Pomeroy home in Strongsville. This book will describe Miller's scientific research and teaching career and how it was shaped by the incredibly rapid and often puzzling progress being made in physics.

Dayton's young life would be significantly influenced by his mechanically talented father, his musically gifted mother, his wealthy maternal grandfather, and by his enterprising uncle, Alson Pomeroy. Dayton was eight years old when his family moved from their farm in Strongsville to the town of Berea, a few miles north along the Rocky River. He eventually had a sister and three brothers with whom he would always remain in contact. His father opened a hardware store, which included a shop where the boy learned much that would later serve him well as an experimental physicist. Charles Miller eventually became a banker and president of a system of interurban electric rail lines. The next eight years would see young Dayton completing his public-school studies followed by two important years at Berea's Baldwin Institute, a liberal, coeducational, preparatory school. This experience in prep school set Dayton apart from the typical schoolboy, putting him on the path to higher education.

Outside of school, Dayton found many exciting projects to work on. After reading a *Scientific American* article about Mr. Bell's wondrous device, patented only two years earlier, Dayton built his own telephone. (He must have built at least two.) The American public was astounded by the telephone, which, they were told, could even speak in Chinese! When he was thirteen, Dayton used the money he earned by growing and selling vegetables to buy an expensive silver flute. This purchase marked the beginning of a lifelong hobby and a passion to learn everything he could about this ancient form of musical instrument. In his teens, Dayton and his father visited telescope maker John Brashear in Pittsburgh. Brashear was a leading authority on the fabrication of precision optical components, and Dayton remained in frequent contact with him as he built a series of astronomical telescopes for himself. Brashear, whom Miller described as his "scientific father" would later play a significant role in Dayton's early career.

On the less intellectual side, young Dayton enjoyed riding his "penny-farthing" bicycle out on the country roads, even down to grandfather Pomeroy's place in Strongsville. This bike, with a four-foot-high wheel up front and a tiny one-foot wheel behind, must have been especially challenging for Dayton, who never topped five-foot-three (1.60 meters). Nevertheless, he was athletic enough to lead the Berea team of young volunteer firemen in an unusual foot race. Each fellow had to run across the field, raise the ladder he was carrying, and scramble up over the top and down the other side.

**Teenage Dayton and his Penny-farthing Bicycle.**

At sixteen, Dayton began studies at Baldwin College, a small Methodist liberal arts school that was just a few blocks from his home. Baldwin, which shared courses with the neighboring German Wallace School, offered classical, philosophical, and literary courses of study. Fourteen faculty members taught about one hundred forty students. Dayton chose the "philosophical program," which included mathematics from algebra through calculus, a lot of German and French, Latin, English literature, physics, chemistry, astronomy, geology, and psychology. During the course of his four years in college, Dayton sharpened his skills at public speaking, a talent that would be central to his entire career. For example, he addressed the school's chapter of the Phrenocosmian Literary Society on such mostly scientific things as bicycles, telescopes, planets, burglar alarms, cremation, and natural gas. One can only wonder what he might have had to say about cremation.

At his graduation in 1886, Dayton stole the show by presenting a lecture entitled "*The Sun*," in which he described the latest progress in solar research. This was followed by his performance with the school orchestra of a solo flute rendition of a Beethoven piece, topped off with a valedictory address about telescopes. The Millers and Pomeroys must have been so proud. This lad was going someplace.

**Miller's Graduation Photograph**
**(courtesy of Baldwin-Wallace University)**

# Chapter 2 Princeton

What then should twenty-year-old Dayton do after college? He clearly had a flair for building scientific instruments as well as a passion for classical music. He enjoyed the support of a financially comfortable family in a suburb of a rapidly developing midwest city. Almost certainly, he could expect to find a teaching career at Baldwin College. But he was not to make a quick decision. Instead, he chose a "time-out," taking a position in Alson Pomeroy's bank. In the dozen years Uncle Alson had lived in Berea, he had not only founded a bank but had become the mayor of the town and, along with Dayton's father, a principal investor in the Berea-to-Cleveland electric street rail line. Dayton could choose any of several careers in his hometown, some of which could make him a wealthy man.

Working in a bank must have been less than challenging for the young Miller for he spent plenty of time building instruments and performing experiments in his father's workshop. For example, having acquired his own silver flute as a teenager, Dayton wanted to learn more about this instrument, not only how to play it, but how it worked. This would become a lifelong fascination that we shall describe in several of the following chapters. The pleasure he had experienced in building astronomical telescopes and his ongoing contacts with the Pittsburgh optical expert John Brashear would finally draw him out of the bank, out of Berea, out of Ohio, and send him off to graduate school. In September, 1887, Dayton arrived at Princeton to begin advanced studies in astronomy. It is likely that Brashear, who was a major provider of optical equipment to the Princeton astronomers, had put in a good word for the young fellow from Ohio.

Miller's advisor at Princeton would be the famous astronomer, Charles Young. Professor Young, incidentally, had spent nine years (1857 to 1866) at Western Reserve College (WRC), in Hudson, Ohio (twenty miles southeast of Cleveland). He, like so many others, had come to the Reserve from New

England. With a degree from Dartmouth, the twenty-two-year-old Young was appointed professor of mathematics, natural philosophy (an old-fashioned name for physics), and astronomy. During his time at WRC, his research was concerned mainly with geomagnetism and geology.

It was not until after Young had left Western Reserve and joined the faculty back at Dartmouth that his career would take off, astronomically. In 1877, Young was enticed to leave Dartmouth to become chair of astronomy and director of the recently inaugurated Halsted Observatory at Princeton University. Young became the world's authority on solar physics. For example, it was he who verified the rotation rate of the sun by measuring the Doppler shift of spectral lines in the light coming from opposite solar equatorial regions.[1]

In 1881, Young had published *the* authoritative book on solar physics, "The Sun." Almost certainly, Miller, the then fifteen-year-old novice astronomer, had read this impressive work, and it may very well have influenced his later decision to study with its author. Remember, the address that Dayton had delivered at his college graduation ceremonies was titled "The Sun." In addition, the new twenty-three-inch refracting telescope at the Halsted promised exciting research opportunities. Miller had read about this first class facility in the *Scientific American.*

Miller's first year as a graduate student (his first away from home) was filled with a heavy load of courses in mathematics and observational astronomy. Most exciting was the chance to work with the latest astronomical techniques and equipment, including the twenty-three-inch telescope. One phenomenon, which Miller studied that year, was light interference. He would spend much of his later research life studying interference effects. (Interference creates the bright and dark patterns that are produced when a beam of light is split into two beams and then, usually by mirrors, recombined. It is one way to show that light is a wave of some kind.)

---

1 The observed frequency of the light coming from the part of the sun's surface, which is moving toward the observer, is slightly increased, and that from the opposite, receding side is decreased. The amount of the frequency shift determines the speed of the source and, in this case, the sun's rate of rotation: about one full turn each twenty-five days.

**Graduate student Miller at Princeton**

Nevertheless, when spring of 1888 came around, Miller decided once again to interrupt his studies and returned to Berea. Whether he was homesick, or family matters called him home, or he was just in need of a break, we may never know. This time, however, he avoided working at the bank and instead accepted a teaching position at Baldwin College. This opportunity to teach at the college level would add significantly to his CV. In addition to gaining experience in the classroom, Dayton completed a Master of Arts in Education in the course of that single year.

When he returned to New Jersey in the fall of 1889, it was time to choose a research project for his doctorate. Does the astronomy student of that, or any, era pick a star out of the sky to study, or maybe a family of stars with certain characteristics? Does he study stellar motions, the spectra of the emitted light? Or perhaps an event occurs in the sky, a supernova, or even a more local and modest event, like a comet? On July 6 of that year, "Mr. W.R. Brooks," as Miller identified him, observed a comet which might turn out to have an interesting history and may be worth further study. The study of "Comet 1889 V" would be Miller's doctoral research project.

# Chapter 3 His Own Comet

Comet 1889 V appears to have been a challenge to comet astronomers for over a century. It was discovered in June, 1770 by Charles Messier in Paris. Early estimates of its orbit had it coming very close to Earth, within six times the distance to the moon. The apparent length of its tail at closest approach was about twice the diameter of the moon, and its light was as bright as the North Star. Experts in France, Russia, and Germany would seek the parameters of its orbit. In 1778, it was the Swedish astronomer Anders Johan Lexell who was the first to publish. (At the time, he held a position in St. Petersburg, where he used the name Andrei Ivanovich Lexell.) Using the coordinates published by Messier, Lexell came up (eight years after the comet's discovery) with a period of 5.6 years. How can that be? It should have been seen in 1776, but it wasn't. Answer: its orbit, that time, took it along a path relative to the sun that made observations impossible. So the cometary scientists, necessarily being patient observers, had to wait for the next scheduled pass in 1781. But this time, it failed to arrive at all! This did not faze Lexell, although there was some public derision of "Lexell's Lost Comet" by people who either had doubts about Newtonian mechanics or thought comets were sent to us as mysterious messengers of some kind. No problem, said Lexell. The 1770 orbit indicated that the comet had passed very close to Jupiter and that it would do so again and again, each time being perturbed into a significantly different orbit. That would explain why it had not been seen *before* 1770, why it failed to show up as predicted in 1781 and, for that matter, why it just seemed to get lost. Until 1889, that is. Professor William R. Brooks was a well-known comet researcher at the Hobart College observatory in upstate New York.[2] Brooks's July observations were soon analyzed by, as Miller wrote it, "Mr. S.C.

[2] It is interesting that Miller wrote "Mr. W.R. Brooks, at Geneva," identifying neither the astronomer's faculty position nor institution.

Chandler, of Cambridge, Mass." [3] Chandler soon published a paper proposing that Brooks's comet appeared to be Lexell's comet. Here's what Miller wrote: "From these approximate calculations it appears that the comet was under Jupiter's control for six months in 1886, its orbit being completely changed from one with a period of about 27 years, in which it could not be seen from the earth, to its present orbit with a period of about 7 years." It had, in fact, passed so close to Jupiter that it sailed within the orbit of that planet's third moon.

Luckily for graduate student Miller, the comet would remain visible for the next several months. Precise measurements of its position in the sky over an extended period should provide a firm footing for future study of this wildly behaving comet, as well as a splendid and timely doctoral research project. In Miller's words: "It will be a great triumph of science if it shall prove possible to calculate the wanderings of this wisp of nebulosity as it is deflected from one orbit into another under the varying forces exerted by the sun and the planets." (Don't all physics graduate students consider their research projects potentially "triumphs of science"?)

Now, we go to the telescope: "the 23-inch Equatorial of the Halsted Observatory, Princeton." Miller's task is to track the comet as long as it was visible to establish the parameters of its orbit. First, one needs a coordinate system. How does one specify a spot in the sky? Astronomers use two numbers, similar to longitude and latitude, to locate an object on the "celestial sphere"[4]. An "equatorial mount" allows the telescope to be rotated around an axis that is parallel to the Earth's axis. In this way, the telescope can easily track an object as it appears to move across the sky due to the Earth's rotation.

On November 14, 1889, Dayton turned the twenty-three-inch toward the comet, centered on it, and wrote down the two coordinates. But it was not quite that simple. First, he must know the exact time at Greenwich (GMT) to within a second. This was provided by an electrical connection to a special observatory clock. He must then record the *exact times* the comet's image crosses two right-angle lines in his eyepiece *and* the exact times an identifiable nearby star crosses those same two lines. Then he must go to the star tables and look up the coordinates of that star, do some subtractions, and write down

---

3 Perhaps, in this instance, it was Ivy League rivalry that precluded a more appropriate identification of Harvard's leading professor of astronomy.

4 The right ascension is in time units: *hours*, minutes, and seconds, and the zero is over Greenwich, England at midnight. The declination is in angular units: *degrees*, minutes, and seconds, with the zero above the equator and plus ninety degrees above the North Pole.

the desired comet coordinates. [5] Over the course of four months, Miller had twenty-five telescope nights with good viewing. Using a total of twenty-one different "comparison stars," he made between five and ten comparisons per night. The resulting table in his dissertation lists GMT to the second, the "comet-minus-star" right ascension difference to the hundredth of a second, and the "comet-minus-star" declination difference to the tenth of a second.

How is a comet's orbit defined? Isaac Newton showed, from conservation of energy and angular momentum, that the orbit of a recurrent comet must be an ellipse with the sun at one focus. Miller's task was to determine the parameters necessary to define an ellipse in space.[6] The hard part in interpreting the data is to account for the orbital motion of the Earth and the tilt of its axis. What does Miller have in his table of numbers? Ideally, he would *like* to have the three-dimensional coordinates of the comet at a few well-known times, all relative to the *sun*. What he actually has is a set of vectors that point to the comet from his telescope, which is firmly attached to the tilted, spinning, and orbiting Earth. He has no direct data on the distance to the comet. It will take some manipulation to arrive at the six numbers required to specify the elliptical orbit in three-dimensional space. The mathematical techniques for doing this were well established, and Miller filled pages and pages with logarithms in the process. He used various combinations from his complete data set to find the best and most consistent estimate of the orbit's parameters.

The obvious check on the calculated orbit is to predict the position of the comet at several future times and wait and look. This series of predicted positions is called an Ephemeris. The full title of Miller's dissertation was "Observations of Comet 1889 V and an Investigation of its Orbit with an Ephemeris." His orbit and predictions were published in the *Astronomical Journal* in April 1890.

Dayton wrote to his father in Ohio, describing his work. "It is this problem which is to constitute my 'Thesis.' It is evidence that it is a great problem when they consider its solution to constitute sufficient knowledge and work for obtaining the Doctor's degree at Princeton. I have practically finished the job, and have spent about 14 hours solid work per day for over 3 weeks on it after

---

5 Nowadays, astronomers use galaxies as standards. They are farther away and don't wander around the sky as much as stars.

6 An ellipse can be described loosely as a circle with two centers. More correctly, it is a closed figure defined by two points in space called the foci and a length L. The length L equals the *sum* of the distances from each point on the ellipse to the two foci. If L is only a bit more than the distance between the foci, you get a long thin ellipse. As L gets bigger, the ellipse gets rounder and rounder, approaching a circle. A comet's ellipse has the sun at one focus.

all the observations were reduced and in shape to work with. The solution is altogether in 7 place logarithms. I have 140 closely written pages of nothing but logarithms." (He didn't exaggerate. Case Western Reserve's archives have his data books: two hundred handwritten pages of numbers.) Miller was awarded the Doctor of Science degree that spring.

A search of the internet for Comet Lexell finds the complete doctoral dissertation of a student at Johns Hopkins University who was competing with Miller. Charles Lane Poor was a student of one of the other luminaries of American astronomy, Simon Newcomb. Graduate student Poor assembled available data on 1889 V, including his own measurements and those of Miller, and did a significantly more sophisticated analysis. Poor took the orbit observed *before* the encounter with Jupiter and tried to calculate the Jovian perturbation, connecting it with the new orbit. Mr. Poor of Baltimore identified Miller's data only as "Princeton"—no mention of his fellow graduate student's name.[7] It is not entirely certain that the Miller-Poor comet was actually Lexell's Lost Comet. Comet 1889 V, known today as Brookes's Comet, after the Hobart College professor, may have been seen in 1896, but not since. It may very well have broken up after interacting with the planets. Miller's painstakingly calculated orbit proved to be ephemeral at best.[8]

---

7 We'll meet up with Charles Lane Poor later in this book when, as a distinguished professor at Columbia University, he and Miller again cross paths as they find themselves at the center of a historical physics controversy.

8 Another internet mention of Comet Lexell describes a 1930s science fiction movie about our comet, once again deflected by Jupiter, but this time on its way to destroy the Earth.

# Chapter 4 Revolutions in Physics

Life at Princeton was not all telescope and mathematics. Among Dayton's friends was an undergraduate student, Will Easton, who shared his interest in instruments and technical devices. Dayton had the opportunity to visit the Easton family home in Princeton. Will's sister, Edith, will be with us to the very end of this book. Another of Dayton's passions, of course, was fine music; and during his graduate-school years, he had plenty of opportunities to hear the most famous and very best. A few hours away by train and ferry was New York City, where the music of Wagner at the Metropolitan Opera would ignite another love affair. Imagine the experience in 1888 of hearing soprano Lilli Lehman in the American premier of *Götterdämmerung*.

Spring 1890: the young Doctor Miller is ready to step out into the working world of physics and astronomy. But, it would seem, not right away. Professor Young, clearly pleased with his student's accomplishments, offered him the Thaw Fellowship in Astronomy, starting in the fall. The plan was for Miller to continue for another year or two at Princeton working with the new spectroscope being installed at the twenty-three-inch by, of course, John Brashear. Miller, now twenty-four, was then free to spend the summer back in Berea with his family. In August, an unexpected letter from Young arrived. Brashear's prisms for the spectroscope were not yet ready. Would Miller please postpone his return to Princeton until sometime the following year? Miller right away began to look for suitable temporary employment. A banking clerkship would not be appropriate for Dayton C. Miller, Doctor of Science, Princeton, class of 1890.

Before joining Miller on his Uncle Alson's street-rail car for the short trip from Berea up to Cleveland, let us take a look at the state of physics in 1890. Motion was well described by Newton's laws for force and acceleration and gravity; theories had been developed for the mechanical and thermal behavior of fluids and gasses; the connections between heat, temperature and energy;

optics and the wave nature of light; the production and propagation of sound (even from flutes). All these things were in quite good shape.

But the most exciting progress involved the new ideas about electricity and magnetism that burst upon the scene in the 1860s and '70s. It had been known for millennia that when rubbed the right way, pieces of amber would repel one another. Needles of iron would move on their own to line up with one another. Electric and magnetic phenomena had joined Newton's gravity in the mysterious realm of *action at a distance.*

During the eighteenth and nineteenth centuries, physicists like Coulomb, Ampere, and Faraday experimented with charges and currents and their interactions. Their experiments showed that something inside a body could "flow" to another body. That something was called electric charge and its motion was called electric current. While it was not known what charge and current were, they could be created and manipulated and measured. The results of years of experimentation were brought together in 1866, in four compact and symmetric equations, by James Clerk Maxwell.

Action-at-a-distance was just too uncomfortable an idea. Instead, the concept of some sort of modification of the space surrounding charges, currents, and magnets provides a more intuitive description of what was going on. These so-called *fields* cause a rearrangement of something that fills all space, something that the ancients called the *aether*. Maxwell's new theory described the connections among the charges, currents, and these fields. His famous equations spelt out the desired relations between electric fields and the charges that cause them, and between the magnetic fields and the currents that cause them. But the fields had even more subtle causes: Maxwell also described how *changing* magnetic fields give rise to electric fields and how *changing* electric fields cause magnetic fields. The mathematical description of this two-way interplay between E and M fields led to an incredible discovery. The equations predicted the possibility of traveling waves which combined the two types of fields and which would move through the aether at one particular speed: one hundred eighty six thousand miles per second. Sound familiar? At Princeton Miller learned about Maxwell's theory and its wonderful prediction of electromagnetic waves that travel through the aether. Maxwell himself described this space-filling aether in a more dramatic way: "The vast interplanetary and interstellar regions will no longer be regarded as waste places in the universe, which the Creator has not seen fit to fill with the symbols of the manifold order of His kingdom."

Miller, as a fresh graduate, became a member of a rather exclusive group, comprising approximately two hundred American astronomers and physicists with doctoral degrees. Only about fifty U.S. advanced degrees in these fields were awarded in the entire decade of the 1890s. Only a handful of independent American researchers were known in Europe—men like Rowland at Johns Hopkins, Gibbs at Yale, Henry at Princeton, Michelson at Chicago. Quite a few others took positions with government agencies, for example, the Weather Service, the Naval Observatory, or the Coast and Geological surveys. "Non-academic" American researchers like Alexander Graham Bell and Thomas Edison were concerned less with electromagnetic theory than with ingenious and profitable applications of currents and fields, such as the telephone and the electric light.

In considering Miller's world in 1890, we should remind ourselves of what was *not* known. Yet to be discovered were the electron, the atom, the nucleus, and even the galaxy. The next decade would be filled with exciting discoveries. Nevertheless, thanks to Maxwell, electricity and magnetism and light were comfortably well in hand. There was perhaps one puzzling issue that had to be straightened out. An experiment performed three years previously, not in Europe, nor in the laboratory of a prestigious American university, but in Cleveland Ohio, seemed to raise some questions about how light moves through the aether. But surely that would be resolved by further experimentation.

# Chapter 5 Case Professor

The ride from Berea up to Cleveland took less than an hour. At Public Square in the center of downtown, Miller boarded the Euclid Avenue electric streetcar, continuing east about three miles to Wade Park. There, amidst what was still largely farmland, two educational institutions had begun operation less than a decade earlier. Western Reserve University (WRU) was originally founded by Connecticut settlers some fifty years earlier at Hudson, Ohio. Most of its early faculty members were Yale graduates. As we mentioned, it was at WRU that Miller's advisor at Princeton, Charles Young, began his teaching career. In the early 1880s, WRU moved to Cleveland and built its great stone building less than fifty yards from the main building of the brand new technical college, the Case School of Applied Science (CSAS). Miller had started college at Baldwin a year or two before these nearby science-oriented schools opened in Cleveland, and he could have transferred to either one. However, the Baldwin school was closer to home and more in line with his interests in music and his family's culture and Berea connections.

**1890 Postcard of University Circle: Western Reserve's Adelbert Hall (left) and Case Main.**

In 1890, the Western Reserve undergraduate college had a faculty of nine professors and five instructors teaching sixty-two men and women undergraduates. It was but one component of the University that included the Cleveland Medical College, a conservatory of music, and a school of art. Its most prominent scientist-researcher was Edward Morley, a physical chemist known internationally for his precise measurements of atomic weights. Morley had started at the Hudson campus in 1869. He regularly took the train to Cleveland to teach some chemistry related courses at the Western Reserve medical school. In 1882, he moved from Hudson to head the chemistry department at its new Cleveland campus. The physics department at WRU was chaired by Francis Whitman, a recent PhD from Johns Hopkins.

Just to the west of the WRU campus was the other hulking four-story stone building, housing the CSAS offices, lecture halls, laboratories, and even dormitories. A faculty of eleven professors taught 103 engineering and science undergrads that each paid seventy-five dollars per year in tuition. The physics chairman was Harry Reid, a geophysicist and another holder of a Hopkins doctorate. He was an expert on earthquakes and glaciers. Reid had taken over the department only a year earlier when Albert Michelson, Case's first physicist, decided to leave.

So Miller, on that day in August 1890, in his search for a one-year position, had the opportunity to visit both physics departments. What is certain is that he met with Cady Staley, engineering professor and president of Case, together with Charles Howe, the newly appointed professor of math and astronomy. These two fellows were delighted with Miller's wide interests and enthusiasm (and Princeton credentials) and quickly decided to hire the twenty-four-year-old. He began teaching only a few weeks later at an annual salary of $600.[9] Miller's assignment was to assist Reid and Howe in teaching introductory physics and astronomy courses for all fifty freshmen and thirty sophomores.

During the next spring-break, Miller, having established himself as an effective and multitalented teacher, made a quick trip back to Princeton, with more than astronomy on his mind. He was most anxious to see Edith Easton again and to present her with the song which he had written. The short but very romantic piece, "*The Audacious Jewel*," ends with a pentameter salute to "the love that beams from Edith's eyes on me." He wanted to tell her about Case and to discuss with her whether to take the post-doctoral position at Princeton, or to aspire to a professorship in Cleveland. They decided on the

9 Today, the starting salary would be around one hundred times more while the tuition is five hundred times higher than in 1890.

latter, and Dayton returned to his position at Case, assured that Edith would soon join him. Back in Ohio, much of his leisure time was spent in composing songs and melodic pieces for small groups. His chamber works, many based on Wagnerian themes, reflected his fervor for that composer's operas.

Miller's career at Case was pretty well-established two years later when he was promoted to assistant professor. In 1893, Professor Reid accepted a position back at Johns Hopkins, and the twenty-six-year-old Miller became chair of the CSAS physics department. He had overall responsibility for the two-semester physics sequence. This included the usual mechanics, properties of materials, acoustics, heat, optics, electricity, and magnetism, with emphasis on laboratory experience in all these areas. The courses concentrated on material that would be most useful for the practicing engineer.

**Dayton's fiancée Edith Caroline Easton.**

In June, 1893, Dayton and Edith were married at the Easton home in Princeton. The young couple went off on their honeymoon trip to Chicago, where the Columbian Exposition was in full swing, in celebration of the four hundredth anniversary of Columbus's most famous voyage. Chicago was *the* place to go that year: wonderful scientific demonstrations, gorgeous pavilions, exotic restaurants.[10] They rode the first Ferris wheel (264 feet high, carrying two thousand riders at a time in giant swinging cars!), were awed by the Tiffany

10 Your author's paternal grandparents, also from northern Ohio, were there that summer on *their* honeymoon.

chapel, heard the Sousa band and the ragtime piano of Scott Joplin, saw a belly dancer do the hootchy-kootchy and Buffalo Bill's Wild West show. All of this was brilliantly illuminated by two hundred thousand light bulbs supplied by the young physicist and master of alternating current, Nikola Tesla. That year, Chicago was *the* place for an unforgettable honeymoon.

Former astronomer Miller was amazed by the display of the enormous tube and mounting of the forty-inch Yerkes Telescope. This project was one of the early triumphs of the University of Chicago's rising astronomer George Ellery Hale. The eighty tons of precision engineering had been built in Cleveland in the shops of Warner and Swasey. We shall see in later chapters how Miller's path would again cross those of both Hale and Ambrose Swasey. Another fascinating semi-scientific device being shown at the fair caught Miller's attention. These were known as Geissler or Crookes tubes. When connected to a high voltage source, these highly evacuated glass tubes would glow with dancing colorful luminous plasmas. No one knew what caused these effects, but Miller realized that these tubes could be useful in demonstrating the wonders of electric currents and fields. So he bought several on behalf of the CSAS physics department.

Dayton and Edith quickly became part of the University Circle community, often participating in musical get-togethers. Among their best friends were the WRU chemistry professor, Edward Morley, and his wife, Isabel. At fifty-four, Morley was twice Miller's age, but for the next fifteen years, until Morley's retirement, the two scientists and their wives enjoyed almost a familial relationship. In fact, for many of those years, the Millers and the Morleys lived in apartments in the same building and regularly dined together.

Miller was impressed by Morley's extraordinary work in the precision determination of the ratio of the atomic masses of oxygen and hydrogen. However, like everyone else, he wondered why, if all atoms are composed of the same basic building blocks, did Morley find the ratio to be 15.879 ± 0.0003 rather than exactly 16. Another topic Miller wanted to learn more about was the work that Morley had done some years earlier, in 1887, with the former Case physics chairman, Albert Michelson. Apparently, there was some controversy concerning their findings.

Miller was hired to teach. But was he expected to do any research? The CWRU physics departmental archives have some fascinating logbooks which offer some clues. One of these contains certificates of calibration for a variety of laboratory equipment, going back to 1891 when Reid was chairman. These included standard measuring rules (manufactured by the Societé Genevoise), resistance coils (Cavendish Lab, Oxford), weights (U.S. Office of Weights and

Measures), barometers (U.S. Coast and Geodetic Survey), galvanometers (Queen & Co., Philadelphia), optics (Carl Zeiss, Jena in Germany), standard electrical cells (Edison Lab).

A second ledger lists all departmental purchases from 1887 until 1903, with itemized expenditures ranging from five cents for staples up to several hundred dollars for batches of Swiss, French, or German instruments. In 1891, for example, Reid bought about $2,000 worth of meters and air pumps and demonstration equipment. In 1893, Miller bought more than a thousand dollars worth from Rudolf Koenig in Paris. Koenig specialized in the design and construction of acoustical apparatus for research and teaching purposes. (Remember, Miller's annual salary was six hundred dollars so these purchases clearly needed the approval of CSAS President Staley and Treasurer Eckstein Case.) This equipment, which covered the entire range of physical measurements, was for use mainly in the teaching labs rather than for research. Engineering graduates would be expected to know how to perform all sorts of precision measurements. In addition, Miller made the lab equipment along with his *own* expertise available (for a suitable fee) to local commercial engineering and technology firms, creating valuable connections in the city. CSAS was growing every year. By 1893, there were eighteen faculty and one hundred sixty-seven students, each paying one hundred dollars per year in tuition and each of them taking at least two years of physics.

**The Case faculty, 1891: Miller at the far right**

At the end of 1895, Miller had the opportunity to do some real physics research on his own. That December, Professor Wilhelm Röntgen of Würzburg in Germany published a paper describing some very bizarre radiation coming from Crookes tubes. As we mentioned above, Miller had purchased a few of these at the World's Fair. Physicists and other science buffs had been playing with these tubes since the 1850s. All they needed to light up a Crookes tube was a good vacuum pump and a high voltage source. Potentials of tens of thousands of volts could be fairly easily produced with an inductance coil in which an alternating current in a primary coil of a few dozen turns creates a high voltage in a secondary coil of a few thousand turns. The high voltage would be applied to electrodes at the ends of the tube, which would glow with shimmering colors. Evidently, something was flowing through the tube. The stream could be deflected by a magnet. It could light up a spot of luminescent paint on the end of the tube. It could even cause a little paddle wheel to spin inside the tube. No one had a clue as to what was "flowing," just that it carried electric charge and momentum. The Crookes tube toy was great fun to experiment with. Case Western Reserve today has a whole showcase of them on display, probably including some that the honeymooners brought back from Chicago. Miller planned to use them to learn more about Röntgen's strange emanations.

# Chapter 6 Penetrating Rays

What had Röntgen found that was so extraordinary? While experimenting with a Crookes tube, he discovered that an invisible radiation came from the spot where the electrical stream hit the glass.[11] This radiation could blacken a photographic plate. It was he who named the unknown radiation "X-Strahlung," x-rays in English. What made it remarkable was the fact that the rays could pass *through* objects placed in its way. News of this discovery was described in newspapers around the world, including the *Cleveland Plain Dealer.* [12]

**One of Miller's Crookes Tubes.**

---

[11] *Proceedings of the Würzburg Physico-Medical Society*, December 28, 1895.

[12] The public were fascinated by the sensational reports, reading newspaper articles about "X-ray opera glasses" for peeping Toms and lead-lined corsets for their prey.

In December of 1895, within days after reading about the new "x-rays," Miller, with Edith's assistance, set up a tube and coil and camera and made some pictures, first of things like metal objects inside wooden boxes and then of Mrs. Miller's hand. Of course, x-ray pictures are not really "photographs" but more exactly are the records of "shadows." Miller had the good fortune to have a twenty-year-old assistant who was an expert at building electrical instruments. It was Dudley Wick's home-wound induction coil that provided the necessary high voltage. Miller soon combined nine separate exposures to create a composite image of his own body—buttoned boots, change purse, and all. Within weeks, similar experiments were being done at other institutions around the world.[13]

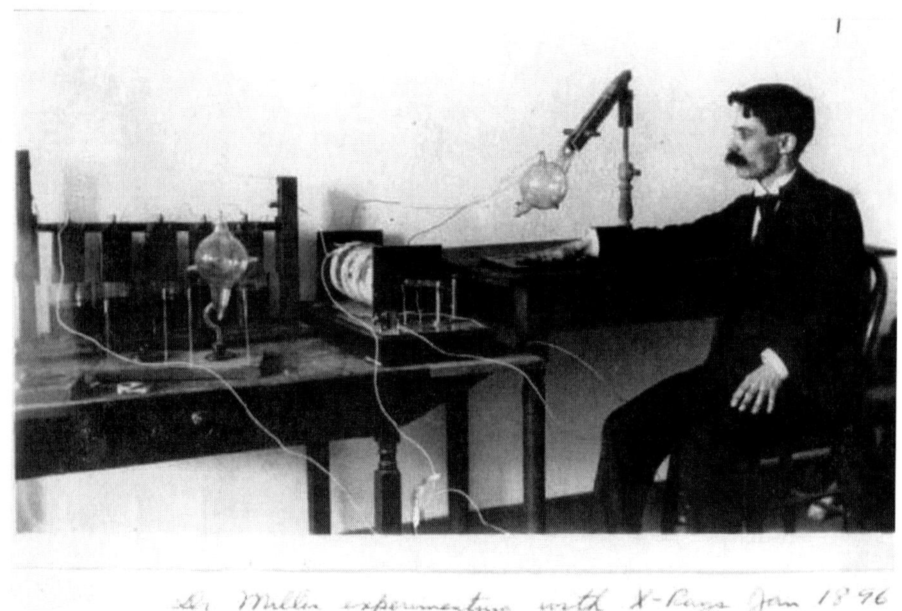


**Miller making x-ray of his hand.**

13 Because many experimenters already had access to discharge tubes in their labs, just who made the first X-rays in the U.S. has been a matter of dispute: Miller's lantern slide is marked "Jan. 1896"; Yale's Arthur Wright is said to have made an x-ray on Jan 27. and Dartmouth's Frost brothers did the same in "late January."

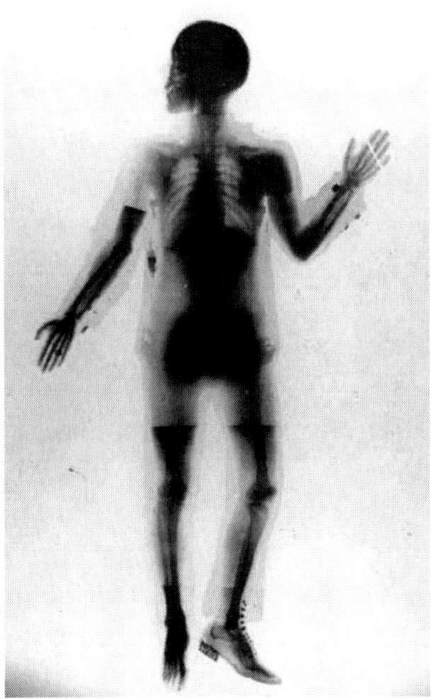

**Composite whole body x-ray.**

By February of 1896, Miller and Wick had improved their "x-ray laboratory." By increasing the voltage and adjusting the pressure in the tube, they were able to make sharper images in shorter exposure times. It was then that they were visited by Dr. George Washington Crile, founder of today's famous Cleveland Clinic. Accompanying Crile was Mr. Maulden, a patient who had a bullet somewhere in his arm, a bullet that the physicians were unable to locate. Miller's x-ray showed that the bullet had lodged among some bones in the wrist. Thenceforth, the Cleveland newspapers published almost daily reports on what Miller and Wick had done the day before. The public, the press, the afflicted, the physicians, the entrepreneurs, the showmen, and eventually the lawyers all wanted to get in on the action.

But none were more excited than the community of physicists (mostly in Europe). How did they interpret this new form of radiation? Could it be another form of Maxwell's waves, traveling like light through the aether but which the eye cannot see? Röntgen himself had shown that the x-rays traveled in straight lines and carried no charge, but they seemed not to be susceptible to reflection or refraction. They seemed to be a form of light with a very *short* wavelength.

Related discoveries came quickly. The German physicist Hertz had earlier discovered long-wavelength radio waves, and in 1896, Marconi in Italy showed how one could use them to transmit a wireless telegraphic signal. Becquerel in France discovered energetic uncharged emanations from radioactive salts, perhaps another type of aether-borne electromagnetic radiation. (Today, we study Maxwell's waves with wavelengths ranging over sixteen orders of magnitude, from $10^{+4}$ meters for radio waves down to $10^{-12}$ meters for gamma rays.) But it seemed that not everything is waves: J.J. Thomson in England showed in 1897 that the "cathode" rays inside the Crookes tubes were not electromagnetic waves but were "charges of negative electricity carried by particles of matter." He named these *electrons*.

Miller was aware of all these discoveries. But the publicity and excitement and especially the interest in x-rays shown by leaders in the medical profession demanded that he pursue and perfect the *application* of this new physics phenomenon. In April, the journal *Science* published Miller's letter describing a variety of images: hands, arms, chest, head, in which he concludes: "The success so far obtained with the arm and chest encourages us to think that still thicker portions of the human body may be studied advantageously, and experiments will be immediately undertaken in this direction." [14]

In April of 1896, only a few months after he began experimenting with x-rays, Miller addressed the Cleveland Medical Society. His lecture appeared as a fifteen-page article in the *Cleveland Medical Gazette*.[15] First, he presented some background on Maxwell waves and the aether and Röntgen's discovery. Then he explained: "This discovery has two distinct aspects. From the scientific standpoint, its main interest lies in the fact that a 'new kind of rays' has been found . . . . The second aspect is that from the popular and practical side, and it is this which interests the people generally." He presented several photos of bullets in hands and broken arms. The doctors were impressed with the technique and quickly saw the value of making an x-ray both before *and* after a broken bone has been attended to. Some of them began to worry about a few cases that had not turned out entirely satisfactorily.

Miller concludes: "It is seldom that a new scientific discovery is so quickly utilized in practical work, and it speaks well for the progressiveness of the medical profession that they have at once and of one accord accepted Röntgen's discovery as an aid in their profession."

The physicians soon found, however, that making useful x-ray pictures was both technically challenging and expensive. Furthermore, they were concerned that non medical (and most often, unqualified) practitioners were pushing the technology on the public. Most disturbing was the inevitability that

14 *Science* **3** 516 (1896).

15 Lecture printed in *Cleveland Medical Gazette,* 1896.

dissatisfied patients would show up at the doctor's office accompanied by a lawyer brandishing x-rays of an improperly set arm bone.

The public was enthralled and turned out by the hundreds at the exhibitions created by Miller and clever young Dudley Wick. These demonstration lectures were meant initially to educate medical personnel, but when the handbills announced "Prof. Miller takes an X-ray negative before the audience, the subject being from those present," the show took on more of a carnival air. In fact, Miller hired a booking agent from Chicago to arrange his appearances. In a letter hyping Miller's talents, agent Caldwell boasted, "Prof. Miller is acknowledged to be at the head in the development of the X-Ray and has performed some wonderful experiments. He has a splendid delivery and the power to hold an audience. This lecture will draw more money with less work than any lecture on the lyceum platform." So all spring long, the Dayton and Dudley show was on the road, all around nearby states. The publicity for the Case School was excellent, and the success of the young physics chairman was greatly valued by the school. Within a year, major instrument makers put entire x-ray systems on the market. Thomas Edison offered a complete laboratory package, including a fluoroscope for immediate viewing.

**X-ray lecture-tour flier.**

There was, as you might have suspected, a dark side to all this activity. Miller early on had noticed a rash on his hand and feared that the rays might be dangerous. Medical practitioners soon recognized the hazard and began to wear opaque lead-lined aprons and gloves. As late as 1902, Miller was called upon to testify in a lawsuit against a dentist whose patient was seriously injured by radiation. *The New York World*, in an article titled "Woman asks $50,000 for X-ray damage," reported that Professor Miller "testified that if Miss MacDonald had been exposed to the x-ray process for half an hour, she must have received a million volts of electricity. 'In my opinion,' said the witness, 'it would have been dangerous and improper to give her such a long exposure as she states she received'."[16] Nevertheless, Judge O'Gorman dismissed this particular case in spite of Miller's testimony. Miller was compensated for his appearance as an expert witness. He reportedly used the money to buy the materials for the solid gold flute he later built.

Sadly, the safety measures were too late for Miller's young assistant, Dudley Wick, who died at twenty-nine, most probably from radiation poisoning. In interviews many years later, Miller described how he remained deeply affected by this tragic loss.

16 Presumably, *New York World* misquoted the witness: a million volts of electricity doesn't really mean anything in this context. It's like describing fifty showers in 120-degree water as a 6000 degree shower.

# Chapter 7 The Physics of Music

In June, 1896, after his whirlwind x-ray semester, thirty-year-old Dayton and his twenty-four-year-old bride Edith set off on their first trip abroad. Chairman and Professor Miller, honored by the company of Case President Cady Staley, had a few "must-visits" in mind. In addition to touristic highlights in Germany, France, and England, he planned to visit Röntgen's laboratory in Würzburg, Wagner's Festspielhaus in Bayreuth, instrument-maker Rudolf Koenig's atelier in Paris, the office of Sir William Crookes in London, and the shop of the flute experts, Rudall, Carte & Co, also in London.

The distinguished physicist, Röntgen, chair of the department at Würzburg University, had just been awarded the £1,000 Rumford Medal for his x-ray discoveries. (Five years later, he would be awarded the very first Nobel Prize in physics.) He and Miller must have had a great deal to discuss, given the incredibly rapid implementation of medical x-rays, and the young Ohioan's role in it.

The couple's next stop was one of an almost sacred nature: Wagner's opera house and unforgettable performances of the Millers' favorite music. Remember, they had often gone from Princeton up to the New York Metropolitan Opera to hear Wagner's Ring and his other "music dramas." Miller's own compositions were most often based on the Meister's themes. What a thrill it must have been for them—not only the music but also the house itself. Wagner had supervised the creation of an acoustic marvel. Years later, Miller would remember this and later visits to Bayreuth when he took up architectural acoustics and was called upon to advise the designers of new lecture and concert halls.

Then on to Paris to see Monsieur Eiffel's towering architectural wonder, to take in a few more operas and enjoy some fine French cuisine, and to visit Rudolf Koenig, maker of superb scientific instruments. Koenig came originally from Königsburg (now Kaliningrad—a city on the Baltic that would later change its address from East Prussia to West Russia). Koenig's laboratory and workshop were in the center of Paris on the Quai d'Anjou. Fourteen years earlier, Albert Michelson had bought Koenig instruments for the CSAS teaching labs.[17]

Koenig's one-hundred-page 1889 *Catalog of Acoustical Apparatus* included pictures and descriptions (in French, English and German) of nearly three hundred pieces of equipment designed uniquely for the study of sound. He had established a reputation in the United States by showing off many of his products at the 1876 Centennial Exposition in Philadelphia. As a result, even today, one can find his acoustics research and demonstration instruments in the showcases and storerooms of many U.S. and Canadian universities—including, of course, Case Western Reserve University (CWRU). As we mentioned, during his first three years at the Case School, Miller bought a significant assortment of Koenig equipment for lecture demos and teaching labs. He was looking forward to meeting the sixty-three-year-old instrument-maker and further exploring his intriguing inventory. While he was there, he ordered item No. 253: "Large apparatus for the study of vibratory movements by the stroboscopic method" 1400 francs. [18]

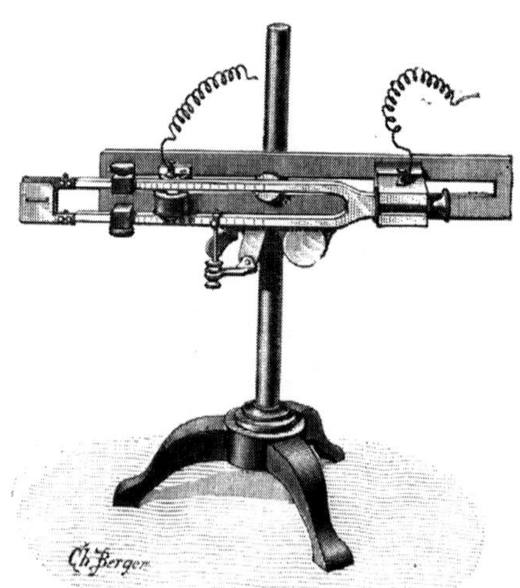


**The Koenig Instrument No. 253.**

---

[17] In 2009, David Pantalony, of the Canada Science and Technology Museum, published a book on Koenig's work: *"Altered Sensations: Rudolph Koenig's Acoustical Workshop in Nineteenth Century Paris.*" Pantalony visited CWRU as a University of Toronto graduate student to examine Miller's papers and instrument collection, contributing to your author's decision to write this biography.

[18] or, if you prefer, "für das Studium der Schwingungsbewegungen vermittelst der stroboskopischen Methode":

Dayton and Edith continued their dream trip, crossing over to London. The only record in the departmental archives relative to this part of their trip describes the purchase of a flute. We have several times mentioned Miller's interest in flutes, but *this* purchase marked the formal beginning of an extraordinary collection. It was especially significant because the flute was made-to-order by Rudall, Carte & Co., according to Miller's specifications. (Partial description: Flute in C. Boehm system. Ebonite with silver fittings. Purchased 21 August 1896.) These Oxford Street specialists in the crafting of high-end flutes had won "The Highest Award" at the Chicago World's Fair, and it was likely there that Miller introduced himself to the firm.

If we were to describe every subsequent purchase of a flute, there would be five per page for the rest of this book. The collecting stage would parallel years of experimentation related to the production of sound by musical instruments. We'll get to that physics part later.

Given all this travel and these purchases, it would seem that Miller had a significant amount of money to spend. He surely supplemented his rather modest professor's salary with income from public lectures, from testifying in court as an expert witness, and from commercial consulting work. It is also probable that his well-off family in Berea helped him. It was time to get back home to Cleveland and teach the CSAS engineers. It was also time to think about what research he might do. Except for a few "expert witness" appearances, the x-ray work was over. Perhaps Professor Morley might have some suggestions for research; perhaps they might collaborate on something interesting?

# Chapter 8 The Michelson-Morley Legacy

The ten days or so aboard the homeward-bound ship gave Miller a chance to relax, to reflect on his and Edith's exciting summer, and to plan for the coming semester at Case. Teaching duties always had priority, but he wanted to get involved in research that would have some basic physics content, something related to the big questions of the day. Of all the people he knew, Professor Morley would be the one most likely to give him good advice. According to the 1900 U.S. census, the Millers and the Morleys had apartments in the same building, a few blocks from the CSAS and WRU adjacent campuses. Neither couple had children. That same apartment house was home for Mr. Eckstein Case, the treasurer of CSAS, indeed the very *cornerstone* of the school's finances. It was a nice arrangement for all, with lively dinner parties, musical evenings, and scientific discussions.

Morley was known internationally for the accurate determination of the ratio of the atomic mass of oxygen to that of hydrogen: $A_O/A_H$. The key word here is *accurate*: in fact, one part in ten thousand. This is as much physics as it is chemistry.[19]

---

19 Morley's measurements were based on the ideal gas law PV = mRT/A. In this equation, P is the absolute pressure, V is the volume, and m is the mass of the gas sample; T is its absolute temperature, and A is the desired atomic mass. The "gas constant" R will cancel out in the ratio of the two As.

**Edward Williams Morley, around 1900**

Morley took two samples of purified gas, one of hydrogen and one of oxygen, and put each into a glass sphere (a few liters). All he had to do was measure the mass, pressure, volume, and temperature of each sample—to one part in ten thousand! A few liters of gas do not weigh very much. But he did it, making him one of the nation's most prominent chemists.[20] As we mentioned before, his result, $A_O/A_H = 15.879 \pm 0.0003$, raised a fundamental question: if all atoms are built from the same building blocks, why was the ratio not 16.000? The world would have to wait another thirty-five years for physics to answer that question.

Morley had in 1895 been elected president of the American Association for the Advancement of Science (AAAS). His inaugural address was titled "A Completed Chapter in the History of Atomic Theory." He would later be elected president of the American Chemical Society. Over the next two years, Miller and Morley coauthored a variety of papers that they presented at professional meetings. These included studies of the coefficient of expansion of various gases, of mercury vacuum pumps, of standard meters, prisms, photometers,

20 Morley, E.W. "On the Densities of Hydrogen and Oxygen and the Ratio of their Atomic Weights." *Smithsonian Institution Contributions to Knowledge*, no. 980. Smithsonian Institution (1895).

camera shutters. Many of these things were related to their respective undergraduate teaching labs.

Most people who have heard of Morley know his name only as part of the couplet: Michelson-Morley. The work that he did with Michelson in 1887 was the basis for research that he would undertake with Miller starting in 1897. To understand this, we need to look at the Michelson-Morley experiment in some detail. To physicists, this experiment has attained almost a mythical status in the development of the physics of the twentieth century.

We saw, a few chapters ago, that Maxwell's equations predict electromagnetic waves and that their speed has one particular value. It seems natural to ask, "speed relative to what?" It was known that sound waves disturb the air through which they travel and they cannot propagate through a vacuum. EM waves also must have something to support them. All of space must be filled with this something. The ancients called it *aether*, the moderns call it *ether*.[21] All light moves at the same speed, relative to an aether, fixed in space.

As the earth travels around the sun at 30 kilometers per second, it moves through the aether. If we could measure the speed of light very accurately, we should detect a tiny difference between light traveling parallel to the earth's motion and light traveling at right angles. It was Michelson who developed a way to do this. He used interferometry.

Michelson sent a beam of light to a "partially silvered mirror" so that half was reflected and the other half passed through. A set of mirrors directed one beam back and forth along a line lying in the direction of the earth's orbital motion. The other light beam bounced back and forth between a second set of mirrors set at right angles to the first. When the two beams were brought together again to be viewed in a telescope, they "interfered" with one another. Where they arrived "in phase," the combined beam was bright. Where they arrived "out of phase," there was darkness. When he looked through his telescope, he would thus see a pattern of bright and dark lines, called fringes. An example of what was seen is shown in the figure.

21 We'll spell it *aether* for now.

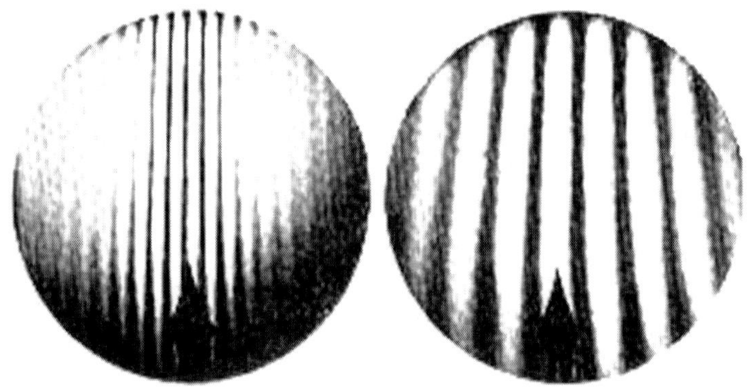

**Interference fringes as seen in telescope.**

Michelson set the whole experiment on a table that could be easily rotated. When the table was turned ninety degrees, the two beams traded directions. If the speed of light depends on its direction, then, as the table is slowly rotated, the relative phase of the two beams changes and the fringe pattern moves across the field of view. From the observed shift in the fringe pattern, one can calculate the difference between the light-speeds in the two directions. Contrary to a common belief, Michelson did *not* determine the numerical *values* of the two light speeds; he sought only to measure the *difference* between them.

Michelson experimented with this scheme when he was studying with Helmholtz at Potsdam in Germany, but without success. He had problems with the smallness of the effect and with vibrations, and was not able to observe the expected "aether-drift" fringe shift.

When Michelson arrived at Case in 1881, he and Morley got to know one another. The young physicist at CSAS and the older, well-established chemist at WRU had offices only a block apart. They traveled together in the summer of 1884 to a meeting at Montreal of the British Association for the Advancement of Science. There, they were introduced by Michelson's former mentor, astronomer Simon Newcomb, to the two leading British physicists of the day, Lord Kelvin (William Thomson) and Lord Rayleigh. Each of these eminent scientists was certain that an aether must exist. According to Michelson's daughter and biographer, Dorothy Michelson Livingston[22], Rayleigh invited the two gentlemen from Cleveland to join him later that fall

---

22 *The Master of Light: A Biography of Albert A. Michelson*, Dorothy Michelson Livingston, Charles Scribner's Sons, 1973.

at a conference at Johns Hopkins. Both Rayleigh and Kelvin were familiar with Michelson's interferometry experiments in Potsdam, and they strongly encouraged Michelson and Morley to collaborate on another attempt. On the train trip back to Ohio, the two colleagues discussed the possibility of working together on an improved aether-drift experiment. Their plan was to enhance stability by placing the optical components on a five-foot-square-by-one-foot-thick sandstone block. Another major improvement was Morley's idea to float the sandstone over a trough filled with liquid mercury. This both reduced the vibration problem and made it possible to rotate the massive stone with only a gentle push. Another improvement was to increase the total length of the light beams by adding more mirrors, making the two light beams travel back and forth several times before recombining.

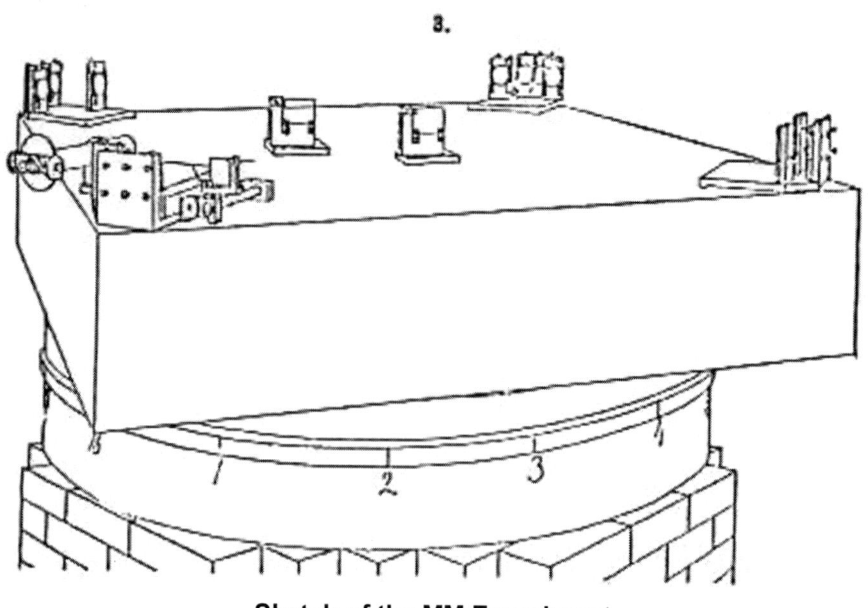


**Sketch of the MM Experiment**

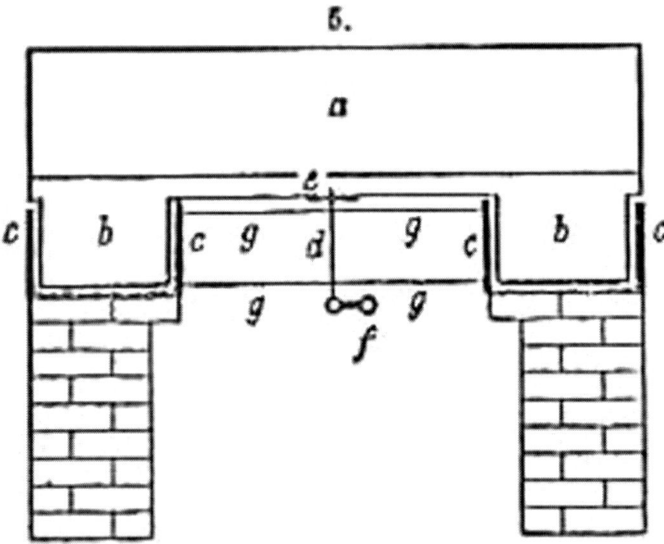


**Cut-away diagram showing how the support floated on mercury**

The expected aether-drift effect would shift the pattern seen in the telescope by only four-tenths of a fringe. Since the slightest temperature variations or mechanical flexing would overwhelm the tiny aether signal, great care was taken to keep everything constant and stable.

In spite of these improvements, the Michelson-Morley ("MM") experiment also failed to show the full expected effect. [23] Michelson wrote to Lord Rayleigh in August, 1887: "if the ether does slip past the earth the relative velocity is less than one-sixth of earth's velocity." [24] For the next two decades, the leading theoretical physicists in the world would be baffled by this result. One remarkable suggestion, made by Hendrik Lorentz of the Netherlands, was that the apparatus literally shrank in one dimension as it flew through the aether!

It would be interesting to know whether the young Dayton Miller, when he was packing his bags to go off to Princeton back in 1887, was aware of the experiment being performed over on the other side of Cleveland.

The *Miller*-Morley collaboration followed upon work that Morley had begun with University of Minnesota physicist Henry T. Eddy. Eddy proposed that the presence of a magnetic field would slightly change the speed of a light wave. (This was not related to the aether-drift problem.) When Morley heard

---

23 *American Journal of Science* 3rd Series **34** 273 (1887).

24 Letter Michelson to Rayleigh August 1887. Rayleigh Archives of the Air Force Cambridge Research Laboratories.

Eddy speak about this at a AAAS meeting in Toronto, he suggested that they might collaborate on an experimental test of the theory. They would use an interferometry technique similar to the MM experiment, this time surrounding the light paths with coils that produced magnetic fields. The AAAS provided funds for the experiment, and Morley invited his new young colleague Miller to participate. After carefully executing the experiment, the three investigators had to report that they found no measurable effect.[25] More important to our narrative than the magnetic field experiment, though, is the fact that this experience of working with Morley would ultimately draw Miller into the aether controversy.

For the next couple of years, Miller was busy teaching undergrads and improving their introductory labs. He began work on a comprehensive manual for them, bringing the experiments up-to-date by the introduction of state-of-the-art instrumentation. He made good use of the generous funding provided by president Howe and treasurer Eckstein Case, ordering equipment from the best providers in the U.S. and Europe, including of course his friend Rudolf Koenig in Paris. The CSAS student body in 1900 had grown to a total of two hundred fifty. Most of these were engineering students who were required to complete the two-semester general physics course: five one-hour lectures and a six-hour lab each week.

Searching for an interesting research project, Miller considered building upon his longtime fascination with musical acoustics, especially the flute. It would be useful and interesting to explore the connections between their physical properties and the quality of their musical sound. Perhaps he could advance the scientific and mathematical approach to the more general study of musical acoustics. But in the summer of 1900, his second voyage to Europe led to a decision to defer the acoustics studies, at least for a while. In June, Dayton and Edith set out to attend the great International Congress of Physics in Paris, this time in the company of their close friends, Edward and Isabel Morley.

---

25 *Physical Review* **7** 283 (1898).

# Chapter 9 Paris, 1900

**Paris in 1900**

Paris in the summer of 1900: what a perfect occasion to visit the City of Lights! The Millers and Morleys were among the fifty million visitors to the 1900 Exposition Universelle. This would even top the Millers' honeymoon trip to the Chicago extravaganza. The French had gone all out to make this a historical demonstration of their arts and science, architecture, and commercial prowess. Many of the buildings we associate with today's Paris were created for the Exposition—for example, the art-nouveau masterpieces of the Gare de Lyon, the Gare d'Orsay, and the Grand Palais. On the technology side, the Palais d'Optique featured the largest refractive telescope ever made. Miller was awed by the forty-nine-inch lens which had almost five times the light-collecting area of the twenty-three-inch he used at Princeton. The two couples must have enjoyed trying out the brand-new Metro underground, the first section of which opened during their visit. To top all of this, Paris was hosting the second Olympic Games throughout the summer. But let us not forget that they were in Paris to learn about the latest developments in the world of physics.

On this second trip to Europe, Miller was in the company of his friend, Edward Morley, distinguished physical chemist, president of the American Chemical Society, and co-author of the controversial 1887 aether paper. Consequently, Miller would have significantly greater access to the major players in the world of theoretical physics than he had at the conference held four years earlier. Miller was thirty-four years old, his colleague, sixty-one. The two travelers' *official* destination was the Congress of Physics, which was to take place from the sixth to the twelfth of August. In addition, Miller planned visits with his friends, the Paris-based instrument-maker Koenig and the London flute-makers Rudall & Carte.

The Congress attracted eminent physicists from Europe and America. So much exciting progress had been made during the preceding four years. The conference was bound to be stimulating, to say the least. With the discovery of x-rays and radio-waves, the range of wavelengths of Maxwell's amazing electromagnetic waves had been extended in both directions: downward to a thousand times shorter than those for visible light and upward to a billion times longer.

Only three years earlier, in 1897, J. J. Thomson in England had published the results of a comprehensive set of experiments on cathode rays. He showed conclusively that the "rays" in the Crookes tubes consisted of negatively charged particles. We know them now as "electrons." By studying their motion through electric and magnetic fields, Thomson was able to measure their charge-to-mass ratio, which turned out to be two thousand times larger than that for hydrogen ions. This established that they had either a much larger charge or a much smaller mass than the ions. (The choice between these two options would not be made for another decade, when Robert Millikan at Chicago would measure the electron's charge and determined that the electron has a mass two thousand times smaller than that of the hydrogen ion.)

Henri Becquerel and Marie and Pierre Curie were among the speakers at the Congress. They reported on their discoveries of spontaneous emanations from a group of very heavy elements, thus adding to the growing list of radiations and particles with mass. The Curies had spent several years learning how to isolate radioactive compounds from Bavarian pitchblende, discovering polonium and radium in the process. In 1898, Röntgen's successor at Würtzburg, Wilhelm Wien, observed a positively charged particle with about the same mass as the hydrogen atom: the particle we call the "proton." The building blocks of matter were falling into place. However, the idea of an *atom*, with a nucleus at its center and orbiting electrons, would have to wait until the following decade.

In spite of all these discoveries and new theories about matter and radiation, most of the participants in the Congress believed that things were quite well in hand and that there was little left to learn about these issues. Even Michelson wrote three years later, ". . . the more important fundamental laws and facts of physical science have all been discovered." But did he mean it? After all, he would spend the next three decades searching for new "facts." For most, Maxwell's waves, transported with the help of the aether, and matter, consisting of some arrangement of positive and negative particles which obeyed Newton's and Maxwell's laws, seemed to provide an adequate description of the world around them.

But still, it would be reassuring if someone could finally and unequivocally demonstrate the aether's existence. Miller and Morley looked forward to hearing and participating in the lively ongoing discussion of Michelson and Morley's failure to observe the aether-drift. Here, thirteen years after the famous but controversial negative result was published, there was still little doubt that something was wrong and that the aether must exist. The challenge was to find out *why* the MM experiment did not detect it. Attendees at the Congress must have been eager to hear Morley's thoughts on the subject. Lord Kelvin, whom Morley had met in Montreal six years earlier, contributed one of the principal addresses at the Congress. His lecture, entitled "Nineteenth Century Clouds over the Dynamic Theory of Heat and Light," described the MM result as a problem that must be solved if any further progress were to be made.

There were several proposals to explain the inability of Michelson and Morley to detect the full thirty-kilometer-per-second shift in the effective speed of light. One of these was the possibility that the orbital motion of the earth in October may have been at least partially cancelled out by motion of the whole solar system. This could be checked by repeating the experiment six months later in April or even better in several different months. The authors mentioned this possibility in their 1887 paper, but they did not follow up on it.

Another suggestion was that the earth drags the aether along with it. Perhaps the aether was trapped within or to some extent impeded by the walls of the stone-walled basement room. To check this, one could at least take the interferometer out of the building, or even better, to a convenient hilltop.

An early attempt to explain the null result of the MM experiment was made by the Irish physicist George Fitzgerald. He proposed that the MM result would be explained if every solid object moving through the aether interacted with it, in such a way that the forces between the object's molecules were modified. The object would literally become shorter along the direction of its motion. To look for this extraordinary behavior, one might attach the interferometer mirrors to materials other than the sandstone used in the MM attempt. Different materials might contract by different amounts.

The Netherlander Hendrik Lorentz picked up on Fitzgerald's idea, but took it to a much deeper level, involving changes in both lengths and time intervals as one compares measurements made in one reference frame with those made in another. What are today called the "Lorentz-Fitzgerald transformations" mark the beginning of "relativity," an approach lurking only at the edges of the 1900 Paris meeting.

One of the world's leading theoretical physicists spoke at the Congress. The forty-six-year-old Frenchman Henri Poincaré, a mathematical physicist, discussed the work of his friend Lorentz the need for an aether and the importance of resolving the debacle of the MM experiment. (It is fascinating to think of all these great minds trying in Paris in 1900 to understand the results of an experiment done thirteen years earlier by two researchers at two little-known colleges in Cleveland, Ohio, USA.) Poincaré's lecture was titled "Relations between Experimental Physics and Mathematical Physics." He spoke of the failure of the MM experiment to detect an aether. He is quoted as saying, "Notre ether, existe-t-il réellment?" (does it really exist?); but he had not made up his mind. He asked where is the light that comes from a distant star during all the years it takes to make the trip? "It must be sustained somewhere, and supported."

Of all the scientists attending the Congress, Morley and Miller were unique in already having much of the necessary equipment on hand and in having only recently used precision interferometry in the magnetic-effect experiment with Professor Eddy. One can imagine them exchanging smiles, knowing nods, and raised eyebrows while listening to the discussion. Most probably, the decision was made, before leaving Paris, to do it all again and surely to settle the issue once and for all. The interest of the physics community was so keen that it should be easy for them to gain the support of their respective institutions.

Sometime during that eventful Parisian summer, Dayton and Edith visited their friend Rudolf Koenig whom they had met four years earlier. CSAS had approved significant purchases of Koenig equipment during the intervening years. It was always a delight to spend time in the instrument maker's atelier on the Île St. Louis in the middle of the Seine. However, this was more than a social call. Miller had already decided to begin a major research program on the analysis of sounds, and Koenig was the world expert on the related instrumentation. His ingenious inventions had already made possible the quantitative analysis of sounds. Unfortunately, Koenig died the following year, and it would be up to Miller and other researchers to pick up where he left off. Miller, in fact, over the next two decades, would become in his own right an acknowledged authority on the analytical study of musical acoustics. We'll describe how he did this in coming chapters.

Most tourists visiting Paris return home with a treasured souvenir, too often a gilded Eiffel Tower. Miller, on the other hand, brought back a gram of radium bromide which he had received from Madame Curie and which he subsequently presented to Thomas Edison. Edison, whose company was a leading producer of x-ray equipment, was interested in the possible application of radium emanations to medical imaging.[26]

Their trip also included a stay in London, which was highlighted by a repeat visit to Rudall & Carte, the flute-makers. Remember, four years earlier, Miller made his first significant purchase of a flute from this same firm. Then, in 1899, Miller had received in Cleveland a *second* made-to-order instrument. These purchases, each of a "Boehm system flute in C," marked the early stages of Miller's study of the relation between a flute's physical characteristics and the quality of its sounds. The high point of this visit to Rudall was the opportunity to try out a solid gold flute. This was a bit of luck, as Miller later wrote: "It had been prepared for the Paris Exposition, but was not being exhibited, as the English exhibits had been largely withdrawn because of the publication of some French caricatures of Queen Victoria."

Miller was interested in how the acoustic quality of the instrument depends on the material used in constructing it. He decided then that he would find a way to build a golden flute for himself and to compare it with those made of less expensive materials.

---

[26] In a tragic analogy with the death of Miller's young assistant in the x-ray laboratory, Edison promptly withdrew from the study of radioactive substances after the demise of his own valued laboratory aide.

# Chapter 10 The Morley-Miller Experiment

It must have been hard for Miller to concentrate on the usual start-of-semester duties back in Cleveland while thinking about what could be the decade's most important experiment. How could he convey his enthusiasm to his colleagues and sponsors? One can only imagine his excitement in describing what he and Morley had heard at the Paris Congress, "Poincaré said this . . . Lorentz thinks that . . . Kelvin insists . . . Lord Rayleigh's opinion is . . ."

The first challenge was to convince Case president Cady Staley and purse-holder Eckstein Case, as well as Reserve's president Charles Thwing, that this project presented a great opportunity for both institutions. One might ask, what does this have to do with *applied* science? Is the aether of any importance to our engineering or pre-med students? Yes, indeed. Technical applications of the recently discovered x-rays and radio waves were already multiplying quickly. It's important to understand how they propagate. Besides, much of the equipment was already in hand and any additional expenses would not be unreasonable. Success would greatly enhance the international reputation of each institution—to say nothing of those of the two professors. Miller and Morley received approval to proceed. According to Miller's ledgers, the "Physical Department Appropriation" for 1900, made by "Mr. E. Case, Treas." was $800. Later, Morley was awarded a grant for the aether-drift experiment by the Rumford Fund of the American Academy of Arts and Sciences.

The new aether-search experiment would take some time to get underway and would be spread over four years. The preparation of the improved interferometer and the accumulation of data would necessarily compete with teaching duties and public lectures. Miller loved speaking to the public about things scientific. He kept a list of the hundreds of lectures he had given, a list that survives in the CWRU physics archives. He gave about ten major talks each year during that period, including some on such topics as wireless telegraphy, or polarized light, or musical sounds, or on the mysterious properties of the newly discovered radium. Only at the end of 1902 did Miller present a paper on aether-drift, this time to the AAAS at their Washington meeting. He and Edith made frequent trips to the east coast, not only for lectures and conferences, but for their own pleasure. Whenever possible, they would take the train to New York, as they had in their Princeton days, to enjoy performances at the Metropolitan Opera. The most memorable of these occasions was the American premier of Parsifal on Christmas Eve of 1903.

Even more demanding of Miller's time during the 1900 to 1904 period was the supervision of the design and construction of Case's magnificent new physics building. We'll describe that project later, but keep in mind that work on the new "Rockefeller Building" and the Miller-Morley aether work ran very much in parallel.

There has been some confusion about *where* the various aether-drift experiments were performed. In 1886, Michelson had set up his laboratory in the basement of the quite new Case Main building, but that building was severely damaged by fire in October of that year. The experiment was moved to the basement of the newly constructed men's dormitory, Adelbert Hall, on the Western Reserve campus. Part of the confusion comes from the fact that the administration building at WRU was also called Adelbert—as it still is today. The dormitory was a few hundred feet south of the main building, along, what else but, Adelbert Road. (The dorm was later called Pierce Hall. It was taken down in the 1950s.) After Michelson left Case in 1889, the large components, like the sandstone slab and its support, were stored in a nearby shack.[27]

It seems that Miller and Morley moved the equipment first to the "basement of the Physical Laboratory" of CSAS, that is, back to Case Main. There they began the construction of an improved design with significantly longer light paths than the MM setup: thirty-two meters compared to eleven meters, an increase in the predicted fringe displacement from 0.4 to about 1.5 fringes. Interestingly, they described their work as a "Test of the FitzGerald-Lorentz Effect" rather than "A Search for the Luminiferous Ether." This more up-to-date description connected their efforts with the most recent theoretical proposals.

In these interferometry experiments, it is essential that the length of each light path remain unchanged to a fraction of a wavelength when the interferometer is rotated. The mirrors must not move relative to one another.

---

[27] Sam Hibben, Case class of 1910, described some years later in a letter to Robert Shankland, how as a freshman he had the job of keeping some order in that "single-room low, wood-frame, unpainted shed, off to the side of the Chem. Lab."

Even the tiniest contraction of the stone supporting the mirrors would change the results. The light path in the 1887 MM experiment was about twenty million wavelengths of the yellow-colored sodium light. The sought-after shift corresponded to only four-tenths of a wavelength. Therefore, a contraction of the total light path of only one part in fifty million would produce the same effect as the expected aether-drift effect.

For the new Morley-Miller experiment, the sixteen four-inch-diameter optically flat mirrors, along with the beam-splitter and compensator, were fabricated in Chicago by Michelson's technician, O. L. Petitdidier. They were attached to *wooden* beams rather than to the sandstone block to test the idea that different materials might contract by different amounts. They used white-pine planks, fourteen inches wide, two inches thick, fourteen feet long, arranged in a cross, attached at their intersection to a cast-iron bedplate. All this was placed on top of the original sandstone block.

**Morley-Miller Interferometer 1904**

The stone block (five feet square and a foot thick) weighed about 1.5 tons. As in the 1887 experiment, it rested on a cylindrical wooden "float" which fitted loosely into a circular trough. About twenty liters of mercury was then poured into the trough and the wooden disk floated on it.

They carefully enclosed the light paths to reduce any effects of air turbulence or uneven temperatures. They chose the dates and times of day for their observations so that the axes of the experiment would be aligned with the earth's orbital motion, combined with what they estimated to be the motion of the whole solar system through space.

Now it was simply a matter of one person walking around in a circle, gently pushing the block, while staring into the telescope at the interference fringes. His partner, watching his progress around the circle, calls out every forty-five degrees for a reading. The viewer responds with his best estimate of the distance from the sharpest fringe to a crosshair in the telescope. From their 1905 paper: "But patience is a possession without which no one is likely to begin observations of this kind. Runs of twenty and thirty turns, involving 320 or 480 readings were not uncommon. A run of thirty turns meant that the observer, who could sometimes make a turn of sixteen readings in 65 or 75 seconds, walked half a mile while making the severe effort involved in keeping his eye at the moving eyepiece without the least interruption for half an hour. The work is, of course, somewhat exhausting."

In spite of all this walking while staring, they kept at it, on and off through 1902, '03, and '04, making improvements along the way. They soon realized that the wooden planks were unreliable: they were too sensitive to humidity and temperature. A colleague from the engineering school designed a steel framework for them. Finally, in response to the suggestion that the aether might be dragged along near the surface of the earth, they moved the whole show up a nearby hill to a site about one hundred seventy feet higher than campus. They set up the interferometer in a building of "very light construction . . . transparent (glass windows), in the direction of expected drift."

Miller and Morley published back-to-back articles in the May, 1905, issue of the *Philosophical Magazine*. The first paper is a long, painfully complicated mathematical analysis of a proposal by William Hicks, professor of physics at the University of Sheffield in England. Dr. Hicks, a former student of Maxwell and a significant player in the aether discussions, had developed an explanation for the null result of the MM experiment. Miller and Morley had to dispose of Hicks's arguments before reporting their new measurements. It took them twelve pages to argue that Hicks's ideas shed no light on the situation.[28] The final results of their own three years' work were then reported in the following

28 *Philosophical Magazine*, May 1905 p. 669.

six-page paper.[29] Here is their conclusion: "We may therefore declare that the experiment shows that if there is any effect of the nature expected it is less than the hundredth part of the computed value. If pine is affected at all as has been suggested, it is affected to the same amount as is sandstone. If the aether near the apparatus did not move with it, the difference in velocity was less than 3.5 kilometres a second, unless the effect on the materials annulled the effect sought." (It is not clear what they meant by "the hundredth part" when the quoted limit was more like one-tenth.)

What a disappointment! They had made so many improvements over the 1887 MM experiment, but their answer, even though they described it as "a definite positive effect," was still no more than 10 percent of what was expected. The aether of Kelvin and Rayleigh eluded detection. Perhaps Fitzgerald or Lorentz or Poincaré or even a younger and more imaginative theorist could explain the results. They did their best, but their work would provide only a footnote to the MM experiment.

29 *Philosophical Magazine*, May 1905 p. 680; *Proceedings of the American Academy of Arts and Sciences* **41** 321 (1905).

# Chapter 11 Professor and Chair

It's not that Morley and Miller spent these years (1900-'06) working solely on the aether experiment. Each was occupied with the design of a new building: Morley, the new WRU chemistry building, and Miller, the new Case physics building. Things were not going very well for Morley. The president of WRU, Charles Thwing, rejected Morley's emphasis on research and on elaborate laboratory facilities in the new chemistry building. The friction between Morley and Thwing had ignited several years earlier when the chemist, returning from a year's sabbatical in England, found all his delicate atomic-weight paraphernalia piled carelessly in a storeroom. Things got worse when Thwing foiled Morley's plans for the new labs.

Sadly, for the institution, for the students, and especially for his friend and neighbor, Dayton Miller, Morley abruptly resigned in 1906, retiring to his Connecticut birthplace after thirty-seven years at Reserve. Here was a scholar who had no advanced training in chemistry nor any graduate science degree, who spent his whole career working mostly alone, far from the great universities in the East. And yet he became president of both the AAAS and the American Chemical Society. His work on atomic weights was respected throughout the scientific world. It was a great loss for the university.

Miller, on the other hand, had the complete support of Case's new president, Charles Howe, and moved ahead on the creation of one of the finest and best-equipped physics laboratories in the world. Successful in carrying out the most important function of a college president, Howe had won the support of oil-tycoon John D. Rockefeller, who gave $200,000 for the construction of two buildings, one for mining and metallurgy, the other for physics. This was rather modest on the Rockefeller scale of giving, compared with the eighty million he had just given to create the University of Chicago. Nevertheless, the $85K for the "Rockefeller Physical Laboratory" was well-spent by Miller.

CASE SCHOOL HAS REASONS FOR ITS SCIENTIFIC HAPPINESS.

**Student newspaper cartoon of the generous Mr. Rockefeller**

The three-story red brick Renaissance style building, with its tile roof and sculpted cornices, is even today among the more handsome structures on campus. Miller wrote, "The purpose of the building is first to provide for the instruction of classes of two hundred and fifty students in general physics, including lectures, recitations, and laboratory work." But Miller made sure that the research facilities were not neglected. Having visited leading academic labs in Europe and the U.S., he had a pretty good idea of what was essential for modern research. More from his description: "There is a balance room, a galvanometer room, a room for mercury apparatus, one for machinery requiring considerable power, a constant temperature room for clocks and seismograph, photometer, spectroscope and photographic rooms, dark rooms, a sound laboratory, a pendulum shaft, a battery room, a mechanician's shop"; "distribution of gas, electricity, hot and cold water, steam, compressed air and exhaustion"; "the research rooms will accommodate 25 advanced students." There follows a full page listing of "special instruments for research," including many expensive purchases from European and American firms.[30] Wallace Sabine, the world's leading expert on architectural acoustics and professor at Harvard University, described Rockefeller as "the best-equipped laboratory in the country." One can only wonder how all this was paid for (more than $100K for the equipment) when the annual departmental budgets were typically $1000.[31]

**The Rockefeller Physics Laboratory**

30 *Proceedings of the Society for the Promotion of Engineering Education* **15** (1907).

31 It is appropriate, at this point in the story, to include a belated memorial note: according to the *Cleveland Plain Dealer* of 9 Sept 1905, a large decorative cornice at the south end of the building, still under construction, collapsed, carrying workers Ed Kelly and Joe Hutter to their deaths and seriously injuring Fred Koreczki and P.H. Whitehouse. It was a sad time for Miller and for Case.

**Rockefeller Main Lecture Hall**

Now that the aether work had evaporated, what might our forty-year-old experimental physicist tackle? Of course, his first duty was to teaching, which included his very popular demonstration lectures for the intro courses. By this time, Miller had some help with the teaching, in the person of a young assistant, Charles Hodgman. A recent BS graduate from Dartmouth, Hodgman would teach physics at Case for forty-six years!

Miller's first book-length publication was related to teaching: "*Laboratory Physics, a Student's Manual for Colleges and Scientific Schools,*" published in 1903 by Ginn & Co., Boston. From the Preface: "This manual is designed to be a student's handbook for the performance of experimental problems in physics." There, " . . . one hundred and twenty-eight exercises are described." All the major areas of what we now call *classical* physics were included: mechanics, sound, heat, light and electricity, and magnetism. The section on light describes an experiment based on his longtime mentor John Brashear's method for silvering mirrors, as well as, of course, experiments in interferometry. That on sound refers to several of the superb instruments made by his friend Koenig. In his list of suggested readings, Miller includes works by Koenig, along with some by Morley, by Michelson, by Western Reserve's physics chair, Frank Whitman, and even by Case president, Cady Staley.

Miller kept the physics curriculum up-to-date. The 1907 catalog describes the senior physics major course, "PHYS 516 "The Electron Theory of Matter." Here are some excerpts: "conduction of electricity through gases, radio-activity, and the electron theory of atomic structure, methods to obtain the ratio of charge to mass for an electron, the possible structure of the atom will be considered." These were cutting-edge topics

Although his duties as department chairman and teacher were a full-time occupation, Miller somehow found time to pursue his interest in musical flutes. In 1901, he had constructed a splendid solid silver flute. In '05, he completed work on one of solid gold. By '07, there were nineteen flutes in his collection, homemade, or bought in London, New York, Boston. Miller now had the opportunity to turn his research efforts to the physics of musical instruments.

# Chapter 12 Unraveling Sounds

His friend and mentor Edward Morley had retired to Connecticut. The exciting prospect of finding the aether had faded. The world of theoretical physics would just have to wait a bit longer on that issue. On the other hand, there were some rumors circulating in Europe of a bizarre claim that the aether problem was actually not a problem! More on that later, in Chapter 14, which describes Miller's return to the aether challenge.

Miller seized the opportunity to explore the physics of musical instruments. It must have been of some relief for him to turn his attention from light waves to sound waves. The propagation of invisible sound is much easier to visualize than the propagation of visible light. There is no question that sound requires a medium. The source of the sound moves the air. The air moves the eardrum. Beyond that, it's a matter of neurology.

A major driving force behind Miller's research on musical instruments was his interest in the flute. A related project was his translation of an 1871 book by the Bavarian expert on the subject, Theobald Boehm. This instrument-maker, performer, and composer, who died in 1881, described the flute as "a gentleman's instrument." His one-hundred-page "*Die Flöte und das Flötenspiel*" (The Flute and Flute Playing) was the bible of flute makers and flute players, and Miller's English-language translation was most welcome. On one of his trips to Germany (probably in 1900), Miller had made the acquaintance of Boehm's family, who encouraged him to undertake the task. The translation, published in 1908, was about two-thirds on construction and one-third on performance.[32]

---

[32] Featured was Boehm's invention of a system of interlinked rods and axles which transmit motions from the fingers to remote tone holes. These hinged metal pieces attached along the length of the flute allow the player to access distant holes with minimal excursions by the hand. Most of the flutes in Miller's growing collection used the "Boehm System."

We return to Miller's laboratory study of musical sounds. *Quantitative* connections between the lengths of violin strings or organ pipes and the pitch of their sounds had been studied at least since ancient Greek times. But it was the *qualitative* properties of the sound that Miller wanted to understand. What makes a "good" violin or a "good" flute? Do subtle features of the geometry change the sound? Does the quality depend on the material of which the instrument is made? We described earlier how impressed Miller was when he first played the solid gold flute at Rudall & Carte in London.

These questions can be answered to some extent by simply listening to the sounds. But can one *measure* the differences? Might the complex sound of an instrument be reduced to numbers? This question would challenge Miller for years.

## Tuning Forks and Beats

The familiar tuning fork has a couple of vibrating tines and a handle. When you strike one tine gently, both tines will oscillate in opposite directions, sending out a pure long-lasting single-frequency sound. How can one measure that frequency? An early way used the phenomenon of *beats*. If you listen simultaneously to two forks whose frequencies are f and f+5 cycles per second (cps, or Hz for Hertz), you will note that the combined sound will warble five times per second as the two tones alternately cancel and reinforce one another. (As in the aether experiments, we are measuring the *interference* between two waves.) Counting the beats gives us the *difference* between two frequencies.

If you use two forks that differ by a full *octave* (frequencies f and 2f), you will hear a harmonious combination sound with no beats. The next step was the favorite of tuning-fork-manufacturers: build a whole boxful of intermediate frequency forks and work your way up, two forks at a time, counting beats for each pair. When you get to the octave fork, you add up all the beats to get the value of f. They actually did this, investing a great deal of money in "tuning fork tonometers." Koenig showed one consisting of six hundred seventy forks at the 1876 Philadelphia Centennial Exhibition. (He tried to sell it there, but no university could afford it.) Once you have a fork of the desired frequency, you can easily create a duplicate fork by making it a bit on the hefty side and then filing away bits of metal until the beats disappear.

The next technique shines more light the subject, literally. Attach a tiny mirror on one tine of the fork and aim a narrow beam of light at it. The reflected light beam will move back and forth. Point that beam at a similar mirror on a second fork oriented at right angles to the first fork, and look at the twice-reflected beam on a viewing screen. The pattern of the combined motion on the screen is called a Lissajous figure. If the two frequencies match perfectly, the Lissajous will be a line or oval which stands still on the screen. If they differ by $\Delta f$, the pattern will rotate on the screen $\Delta f$ times per second. This is a standard technique for matching two frequencies.[33]

If one attaches the second mirror to a rotating shaft instead of to another fork, the twice-reflected light makes a beautiful sine-wave pattern on a viewing screen! If you know how fast the mirror is turning, then you know how long the beam takes to sweep across the screen. By counting the waves across the screen, you can determine the frequency.

Koenig built a clock whose delicate escapement was driven directly by the tiny oscillations of a two-foot long 120-Hertz fork. By comparing his clock with astronomical standard clocks, he could determine the exact frequency of the fork. The fork-clock which Miller later bought is still on display in the Rockefeller building.

## The Manometric Flame

Counting beats, spinning mirrors, tuning-fork-clocks—all these were nice for measuring times and frequencies but still not enough to look at complex sounds. An early step in this direction was taken in the 1860s when Koenig invented the manometric flame. In this device, the sound causes a diaphragm to vibrate (as in Mr. Bell's invention). The diaphragm has its back to a small chamber through which gas is flowing. The gas feeds a tiny flame whose size varies in response to the slight changes in gas flow. When you look at the image of the flame in a rotating mirror, you see much more than sine waves. You see a great deal of repeating structure in the sound wave, structure resulting from the combining of many frequencies. These are the *overtones* that Miller was after. The figure shows three flame traces: high and low frequency sounds and the sum of the two. Koenig described what he was trying to create in his 1865 catalog: "methods for observing the vibration of sounds without assistance from the ear." For the next thirty-five years, he continued to craft new inventions for this purpose.

---

[33] In his 1882 speed-of-light measurements at Case, Michelson used the Lissajous technique to compare the rate of a spinning mirror with the frequency of a standard tuning fork.

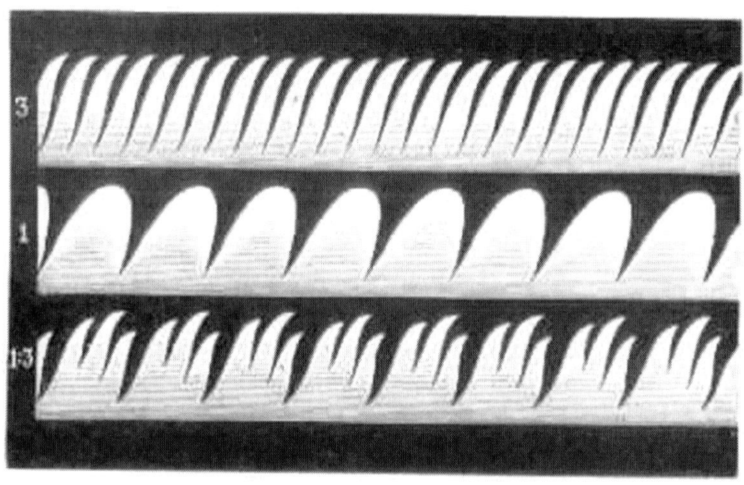


**Manometric flame patterns for two frequencies and their sum**

Hermann von Helmholtz was both physiologist and physicist; he explored the connections between sound as a disturbance in the air and sound as it is delivered to the brain. In his 1862 book "*On the Sensations of Tone as a Physiological Basis for the Theory of Music*," Helmholtz stressed the role of beats in the listener's evaluation of a complex sound. This four-hundred-page tome examined every aspect in the production, measurement, analysis, and appreciation of musical and even spoken sounds.

Helmholtz, like his younger competitor Koenig, created devices to quantify the properties of musical sounds. He designed resonators, beautiful shiny brass spheres or cylinders, which respond to particular frequencies. If you hold one up to your ear, like the seashell you found on the beach, and if the complex incoming sound "contains" that component, the resonator amplifies it. Helmholtz built whole arrays of resonators in his effort to analyze complex sounds. Koenig built a fine-looking device using six Helmholtz resonators connected to six little manometric flames whose reflections dance together in parallel traces reflected by a single rotating mirror. The CWRU physics archive has the one that Miller bought. It makes an interesting demonstration but does not do much for quantitative analysis.

## The Phonodeik

In 1908, Miller invented the *phonodeik*. The idea was similar to the manometric flame, but instead of a dancing flame controlled by a moving diaphragm, the phonodeik uses a narrow beam of light reflected from a tiny mirror connected to the diaphragm.[34] The figure shows Miller's diagram of the phonodeik. The sound enters the collecting horn and strikes a thin mica diaphragm. A tiny thread attached to the center of the diaphragm wraps once around a sapphire-jewel-mounted shaft on its way to a spring that holds the string in tension. A one-millimeter-square mirror is glued to the shaft. A very narrow beam of light is reflected by this mirror toward a camera with film moving as fast as one thousand feet per second. The sound moves the diaphragm which pulls the thread which turns the shaft which rotates the mirror which directs the light to the moving film. The results are astounding!

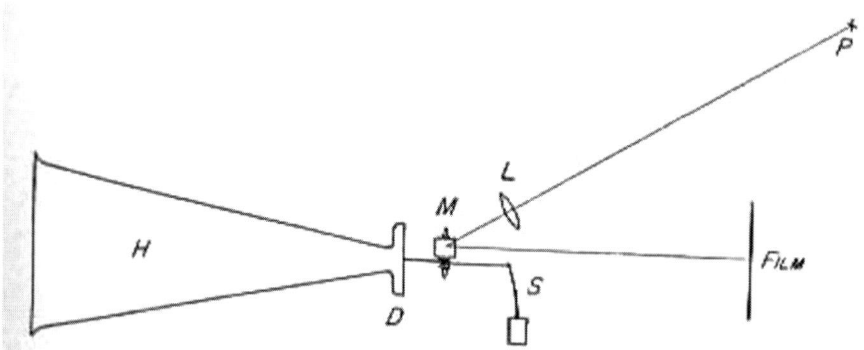


**Phonodeik schematic. Horn, Diaphragm, Mirror, Spring, Point-light-source, Film.**

Miller worked hard to perfect his invention. A necessary condition for good "sound images" was the elimination of external vibrations, a challenge he had confronted in the earlier aether experiments. In anticipation of this need, he equipped his new physics building with several solid masonry columns reaching from bedrock upward to the second and third floor laboratories and lecture-hall counters.

34 The name "phonodeik," coming from the Greek for "to show sound," was suggested by Morley; it was reportedly pronounced phono-deek, not dike—in spite of what teutonophones might prefer.

**Phonodeik lab with vibration-free platform**

Phonodeik collecting horns of various sizes and materials, as well as diaphragms of different diameters and thicknesses were tested to find the best results. It was important that the mechanical parts should not over-emphasize some frequencies or be insensitive to others. To calibrate the photographic images, a timing mark was projected onto the film by a second beam of light bouncing off a mirror on a tuning fork.

Phonodeik traces of all types of sound were made: flutes, clarinets, saxophones, violins, pianos, clanging bells, spoken vowels, exploding firecrackers. Simple inspection of the traces could yield rough estimates of the relative strengths of the fundamental tone and as many as a dozen overtones. Just looking at the picture, one can get some sense of the sound: the smooth flute, the reedy clarinet, the rich saxophone, the clanging chimes.

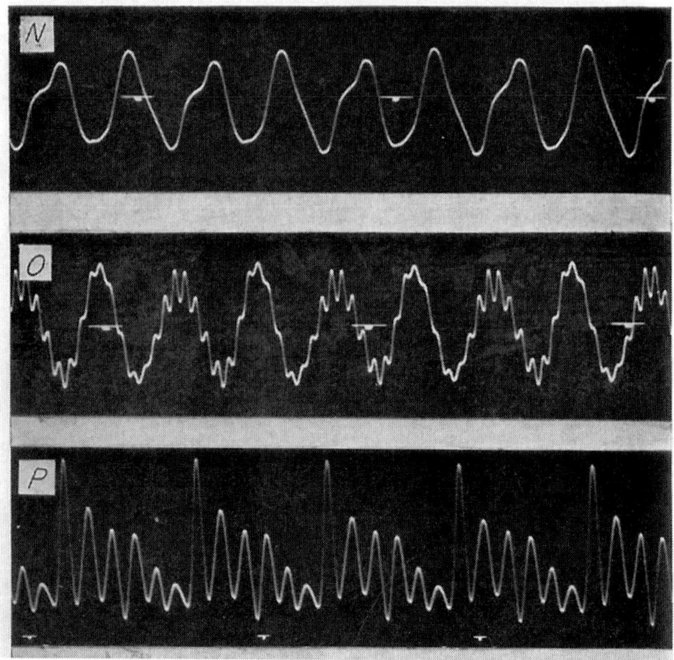


**Phonodeik traces of vowel sounds: oo, ee, ah** Vowels

Another, and even more complex, "wind instrument" that interested Miller was the human voice, and in particular, the persistent tones of the spoken vowels. What makes the difference between the ee sound in meet and the oo sound in moot? Just pronouncing these sounds gives us a clue: the ee sound has more high frequency overtones than the oo sound. For the ee, the tongue goes up and makes a small resonant chamber at the top of the mouth; for the oo, the tongue moves downward, leaving a larger and lower-frequency resonating volume.

Helmholtz had earlier looked into the vowel question. By using his resonators, he was able to estimate the amplitudes of the first few harmonics of each vowel sound. He then built a machine consisting of electrically driven tuning forks and resonators, which he could program to imitate pure vowel sounds. [35]

[35] The University of Toronto owns one of Helmholtz's *vowel synthesizers*, and I was invited to try it out. It might take a bit more practice to "hear" the synthesized vowels rather than just the drone of a chorus of tuning forks.

## Harmonic Analysis

Musical and vowel sounds consist of a mix of frequencies but not of just random frequencies. The sum of the components must repeat in time to make a persistent tone. A violin playing a middle C (256 Hz) produces overtones coming from "sympathetic" vibrations of the string, the wood, the air inside, etc. A flute playing the same note decorates the 256 Hertz with a different set of overtones, coming largely from vibrations of the air inside the tube. A soprano singing "oo" at 256 Hertz sounds very different from a tenor doing the same.

In the 1880s, Helmholtz used his ears and his resonators to approximate the amount of each component. In the 1890s, Koenig did so by looking at the size of the repeating bumps in his dancing flames. In 1910, Miller used his phonodeik to create detailed photographic records of the waveforms. By examining the traces on the films, he could estimate the amplitude, that is, the amount of energy associated with each component and compile a list of "ingredients." This was almost impossible to do by hand as the little wiggles of the overtones ride in a complicated way on the backs of the lower frequencies. But technology intervened in the form of a remarkable machine, called the Henrici.

This machine, invented by mathematician Olaus Henrici, makes use of Fourier analysis. Fourier's idea is that any repeating wave form can be expressed as the sum of sine waves with frequencies f, 2f, 3f, etc. The Henrici allows one to determine the amplitude of each component. The machine which Miller bought from instrument-maker A. Coradi in Zurich would be used at Case over the next four decades for the analysis of wave forms of all types by Miller and his successors.

Briefly, the Henrici "harmonic analyzer" consists of a drafting table where you place a blow-up of the phonodeik image and a mouse-like device which you move carefully along the curve. The mouse is connected by taut strings to an array of pulleys and rotating spheres. Little disk-shaped numerical counters are pressed up against the equators of the spheres. After you have traced out one complete cycle of the curve, the counters are read out. These numbers gave an accurate measure of the amount of each component.

The Henrici gives you not only the amplitudes of up to thirty harmonics but also their relative *phases*, that is, the shifts of the component sine waves relative to one another. Koenig was convinced that the phases are important to the quality of the sound. He even built a double siren with which he could combine two pure tones while changing the relative phase between them.

Now, with the Henrici set up in his lab in Rockefeller, Miller began extracting numbers from his phonodeik pictures, hoping to discover the origins of the subtle differences in the tones of musical instruments and perhaps even to quantify the sounds of the spoken vowels. There had long been a disagreement among the experts as to whether the sounds of musical instruments are influenced by the type or density or thickness of the material, as in the wooden versus golden flute comparison. Helmholtz insisted that the sound depended only on the geometry of the air space and not on the surrounding material. Koenig felt that it was more complicated than that.

In a 1909 article in *Science*,[36] Miller described his measurements of organ pipes and flutes having walls of different thicknesses and densities. He was certain that the sound waves from thin walled, high-density pipes were the richest in harmonics. His reaction to the golden flute now had some quantitative physics support. His paper concluded: "the effect of the material on tone quality of wind instruments certainly is not a fable."

While this sort of information would be useful for makers of all kinds of musical instruments, other researchers were interested. For example, the manufacturer of phonograph record players, of the type then found in almost every American home, could compare the waves coming from their speaker horns with the original sounds in the recording studio.

The numerical answers from the Henrici began to pile up. Miller demonstrated how precisely the analyzer could measure amplitudes and phases by scanning waveforms of known composition. A simple example is the zigzag or saw tooth curve, for which the Fourier components are known exactly. The first four terms (in arbitrary units) are 127.32, 63.66, 42.44, and 31.83. The Henrici counters read 127.30, 63.55, 42.47, and 31.85. That's pretty amazing for a big, bulky contraption built of wires and pulleys and turning spheres.

## The Harmonic Synthesizer

Finally, there is yet another machine. Miller wanted to be sure that the amplitudes and phases coming from the Henrici do indeed describe the source waveform. He set his students the task of calculating points along the curve, and then plotting them on paper, to be compared with the original. He soon found that this could be done automatically. Lord Kelvin, at Glasgow in 1872, had built a machine which accurately predicted the tides, which the press called the "tide prophesizer." Tides depend not only on the moon but on the

[36] *Science*, **29** 161-171 (1909).

sun and the location *on* the earth. Kelvin's machine combined ten different harmonic components to produce a plot of the expected times and heights of the tides.

This was exactly what Miller needed to reconstruct his sound wave forms from their harmonic components. He designed a "harmonic drafting machine," which is essentially the opposite of the Henrici.[37] It was built entirely by his machinist crew in the Rockefeller shop. It consisted of a set of pulleys of various sizes, connected by cables to a pen which drew the curve on a large piece of paper. One had *only* to position a series of set-screws on the pulleys to *feed in* the amplitudes and phases. His students agreed that tightening twenty or thirty screws was much easier than looking up all those sine's and logarithms. The second figure below shows Miller standing at the operator's end of the enormous device.

**The Henrici harmonic analyzer**

[37] A 32-Element Harmonic Synthesizer, *Journal of the Franklin Institute*, pp. 51-81 (Jan 1916).

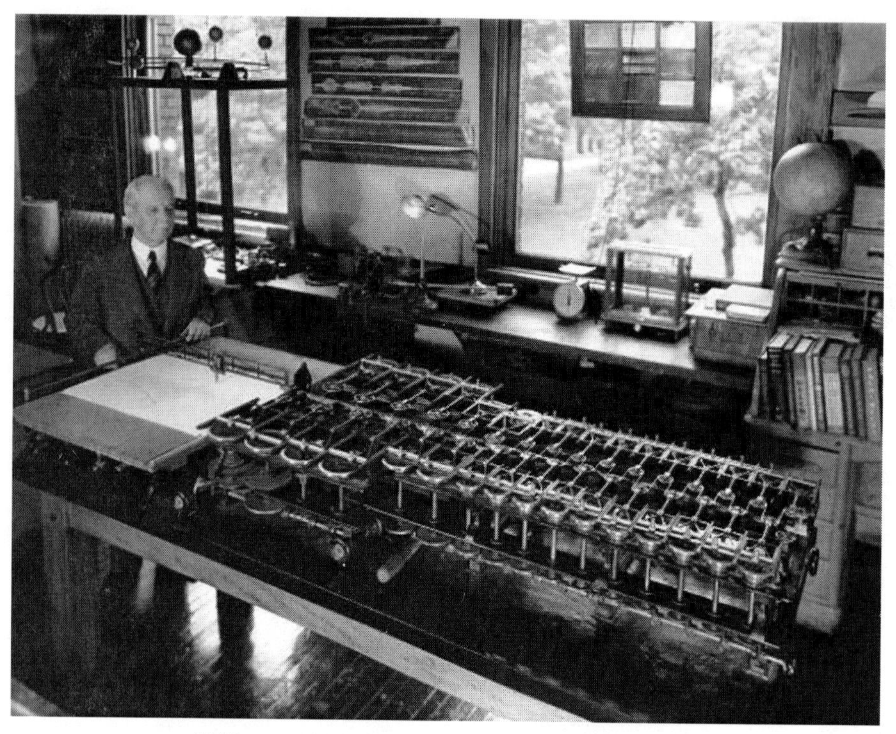

Miller and his harmonic drafting machine

# Chapter 13 Taking Acoustics to the Public

Miller greatly enjoyed telling the public about x-rays in his popular lectures back in the late 1890s. His charm and humor and ability to explain science to a general audience made him a sought-after speaker in the U.S. and abroad. Twenty years later, the now middle-aged Miller had another story to tell, one based on the visualization of sounds. Indispensable to the presentations was his new “portable phonodeik.” This version of his invention included a high-powered arc lamp and mirrors and lenses which allowed him to project live moving traces of sounds on a large screen. Scientists and the general public and everyone in between were delighted by the intriguing show.

His first major formal lecture on the analysis of sound was given in Boston at the 1909 Annual Meeting of the AAAS. Between 1910 and 1920, he and Edith traveled to colleges and conferences, in the U.S. and in Europe, captivating audiences with their visible sounds. Miller’s own list of appearances records over ninety large public lectures, with audiences ranging from fifty up to a thousand, at destinations like Purdue, Stanford, Pittsburgh, Berkeley, Stevens, Cornell. A typical lecture would begin with some acoustics technology and history, followed by the projection of a tuning fork’s beautiful pure sine wave. He would then explain how most sounds consist of combinations and overtones of such waves. He then worked his way up through melodious instruments, startling noises, spoken vowels, songs by volunteer singers from the audience, and often ending up by projecting the recorded voices of opera stars like Enrico Caruso and Luisa Tetrazzini.

One favorite of the audience was the tuned sticks. Miller had bought a set of wooden sticks from the German successor to Koenig, Max Kohl of Chemnitz.

The CWRU physics department still owns several dozen of them. Each stick is eight inches long, an inch wide, and between one-fourth and one-half inch thick. The only difference between two sticks is thickness and type of wood. When dropped on the floor, each stick emits a dominant frequency, do re mi fa . . . up to the octave. Miller would first drop a handful of sticks to make a general clatter and then, dropping one at a time, he played out the tune of Home Sweet Home.

## Architectural Acoustics

Another component of experimental acoustics, pioneered by Harvard's Wallace Sabine, was the study of the properties of large halls used for lectures or musical performances. The key quantity is *reverberation time*, the amount of time a sound spends bouncing around the hall before dying away. This depends on the geometry of the room, the reflections from the walls and ceiling, and the absorption of the sound by the contents of the room, including the audience.[38] Miller's audiences burst out in laughter when he told them that, compared with an open window, women absorb 54 percent of the incident sound while men absorbed only 48 percent. Years later, Miller would become very much in demand as an architectural acoustics consultant.

Wherever he went, the press picked up on his remarkable lectures. *The New York Times* headlined: "Did you ever see a noise?" *The New York Globe*: "Can Photograph Sound—He Says." *The Pittsburgh Gazette*: "Audience Sees Picture of Applause."

As his research in Cleveland progressed, Miller added more material to his presentations. He found, for example, in his study of the vowel sounds, that sopranos, reaching for a high-pitched note can easily sing ahh, but not ohh. This often makes them hard to understand. He argued that because the most "relaxed" vowel sound is ahh, any infant will begin to talk using ahh sounds. *The New York Times* headline: "Solves Origin of Papa and Mama."

As Helmholtz had done years before, Miller experimented with a set of tuned organ pipes, which could emit the proper proportions of tones and overtones, as specified by a recipe found with the Henrici. The goal was to create a more advanced form of the Helmholtz "vowel synthesizer," something which would eventually be accomplished with modern computer technology.

---

[38] The modern unit of sound absorption, the sabin, is named after Professor Sabine.

## Acoustics Consultant

As the best-known American spokesman for analytical acoustics, Miller found much more to do than entertain the public on the lecture circuit. There were many areas, technical and commercial, where the control of sound was central. Miller's phonodeik-Henrici combination had a surprising number of applications, some of which would provide "consultant compensation," that is, money. Miller's travel budget and the rather large investment he continued to make in his flute collection were beyond the reach of a college professor.

Miller was invited by a physicist at McGill University in Montreal to bring his expertise to Canada for a rather different acoustics challenge. The Canadian government had initiated a formal study of fog horn signals. The phonodeik was set up at Father Point, way up near the mouth of the St. Lawrence. The resulting photographic traces were then analyzed with the help of the Henrici. The moans of the horns' warning signals were composed, of course, of many overtones, some of which traveled further than others. Miller presented his results to the Royal Society of Canada in the form of numerical tables of signal strength versus frequency and distance. (F below middle C, around 174 Hertz, seemed to carry the best.)

Miller became interested in player pianos. Various forms of these instruments could be found in typical homes in the U.S. and Europe. The music was recorded on perforated paper rolls. The more sophisticated models had self-contained internal players which combined electric and pneumatic switches and valves to impel the hammers against the strings. Some bizarre looking players were 100 percent automatic, having no keyboard at all. More advanced models could imitate the timing, touch and dynamic nuances of the original performance. Thousands of titles were produced by the leading pianists of the day, both classical and jazz. For two decades, the "Pianola" was the king of home entertainment, when most homes had a piano, and half of these had built-in players.

As a hobby, Miller learned to cut player-piano rolls by hand, combining the full lyrical and instrumental scores of Wagnerian operas into integral pieces to be played at home on a specially prepared piano. He and Edith often entertained their friends at musical house parties, featuring these creations as well as their own live performances on flute and piano.

The Pianola provided another opportunity for phonodeik analyses: the sounds of the original performance and those produced by the player pianos could be compared. The Miller archival files include a full page advertisement in the *New York Times* for the Aeolian Co., the world's largest Pianola manufacturer. Featured in the ads are large pictures of Miller's phonodeik wave tracings, testimony to claims of the highest fidelity. A similar consulting opportunity later came from manufacturers of phonograph machines and radios with loudspeakers. The photograph shows some of these set up in the phonodeik lab at Case.

**Phonographs in the phonodeik lab**

In the summer and autumn of 1912, Miller and his wife Edith were once again touring Europe. Universities in Cambridge, Dundee, Paris, Berlin, and London invited Miller to deliver his now-famous Pictorial Sound lecture. One highlight of their stay was a visit to the South Kensington Museum to see the Kelvin tide predictor. While in London, Miller received an exciting letter from Berlin. It seemed that Kaiser Wilhelm had heard about the phonodeik lecture, and he invited Miller to return to Berlin to deliver it at the Royal Palace. Miller responded that he would be delighted to do so at a later date, but the onset of the European war kept that visit from happening.

Lord Rayleigh, the world's leading expert on theoretical acoustics, invited Miller, the world's best-known popularizer of experimental acoustics, to visit him at his home. Rayleigh, recipient of the Nobel Prize eight years earlier, had for example developed the "duplex theory" of sound reception, which described the ability of a person to determine the direction of a source of sound by processing the tiny differences in the arrival times at the two ears. Miller brought his phonodeik with him. One can imagine what a fine time the forty-six-year-old American and the seventy-year-old Englishman had playing with it, as their patient spouses looked on over their teacups.

The year 1912 was an uneasy time in Europe. No one knew whether, where, or when war would break out. Germany was threatening French interests in Morocco. Turkey was fighting Italy over Tripoli. Everyone was fighting everyone else in the Balkans. France and Russia were getting ready to take on the Germany-Austria-Italy alliance. Great Britain was deciding whether they were with the Germans or with the Russians. The American tourist in Europe, traveling from country to country, must have felt the growing tensions. What's more, the sinking of the Titanic earlier that year was certainly on their minds as they sailed home.

## The Lowell Lectures

In January of 1914, Miller was invited to speak at the prestigious Lowell Institute Lecture Series in Boston. This was no simple undertaking; it involved two-hour lectures each Tuesday and Friday evening, four weeks running. It was in effect a mini-course in acoustics. The program reads much like this chapter: types of sound waves, recording with the phonodeik, analysis with the Henrici and synthesis with the "Kelvin," requirements of the phonodeik horn and diaphragm, tone quality, musical instruments, vowels, synthesis, and reproduction of speech. The Boston newspapers followed each lecture with detailed and glowing articles, describing the enthusiasm of the audience of five hundred science enthusiasts. The material presented in the Lowell lectures provided the substance of Miller's book "The Science of Musical Sounds" published soon after by Macmillan. While in Boston the Millers were the guests of architectural acoustics expert, Wallace Sabine and his wife. Sabine and Miller had become close friends and would remain in professional contact for many years.

In June of 1914, all hell broke loose in Europe. There would be no more leisurely tours or friendly lectures. The heir apparent of Austria was assassinated; and within months, armies were rolling across the continent. The troops were soon stopped in their tracks, and the cruel horror of trench warfare began. It was not until July of 1917 that the American forces arrived in France, tipping the scales in favor of the allies, helping to end the war sixteen months later.

## The Sounds of Guns

In the spring of 1918, Miller was invited to assist the U.S. government in researching the properties and consequences of the sounds of heavy artillery.

Taking a leave of absence from Case which would last for over eighteen months, Miller set up his equipment at Sandy Hook, NJ, and at other gunnery test sites along the east coast. The study was part of a larger federal project on the causes and effects of "shell shock." Soldiers forced to man stations all along the war fronts in Europe had to put up with the painfully loud sounds of the big guns of both armies. Not only did many of them suffer physical damage to their hearing, but a large number sustained more serious brain injuries.

Miller was asked to quantify the intensity of the sounds at different distances and directions from a variety of ordnance. Placing pressure sensors at various locations, he collected the electrical signals and used them to make simultaneous tracings on a moving paper strip, a technique similar to his phonodeik recordings. At the heart of the setup were "string galvanometers," sensitive current detectors developed originally by the inventor of the electrocardiograph. The tracings look like an EKG, with a sharp jump at the arrival time from each sensor. Some of the artillery pieces were enormous. The fourteen-inch diameter shell standing next to Miller in the photograph was propelled by a "rifle" with a barrel over one hundred feet long. [39]

**At the Sandy Hook artillery range**

[39] *Physical Review* **17** 255 (1921).

Although Miller was away from campus, on and off for a year and a half, he didn't miss much. Most research projects were deferred during the war and teaching was pretty much limited to the bare essentials. In August of 1918, the age of the military draft was lowered from twenty-one to eighteen, pulling many of the students away from their studies. A compromise arrangement followed with the establishment of Student Army Training Corps units at both Case and Reserve. On the plus side, the government paid for tuition, food, and shelter. This allowed the Case enrollment to double to eight hundred. On the minus side, SATC students were required to finish their degree requirements in two years time. They spent so much of their day marching around campus that there was nowhere nearly enough time for learning. The faculty was frustrated by the situation.

Miller kept a variety of ledgers and diaries, many of which are in the CWRU physics archives. Here are some entries for 1918: "Oct 1-4 S.A.T.C. schedule of class in 7 divisions with 4 recitations each, and one general lecture. Looking for new Instructor. Oct 5-Quarantine on account of Influenza, all college work stopped. Research work practically abandoned. Nov 11. Have secured two new Instructors . . . making four in all . . . with this help, my own time is wholly available for research." He then added two words, underlined: "Armistice Day!" The World War had ended. The next day, he was working on a new shutter for the phonodeik.

That same year, English astronomer Arthur Eddington traveled to Principe, a Portuguese island off the west coast of Africa, to take some pictures of a solar eclipse or, more precisely, to take some pictures of a few stars *during* a solar eclipse. After the photos had been carefully measured back at the University of Cambridge, the results were announced in the headlines of newspapers all around the planet.

# Chapter 14 New Theories Challenge Old Physics

By 1919, fourteen years had passed since Miller and Morley had tried their hands at detecting the aether. Their final round of data-taking had taken place in 1905 in an improvised laboratory/shack up the hill from Case. They reported a "definite positive effect" of about one tenth of that expected from the thirty-kilometer-per-second orbital motion of the earth. The question of the existence of the aether, or at least of why the observed shift was so small, remained unanswered.

Today, physics historians call 1905 the *Annus Mirabilis*, in recognition of the publication that year of four papers by the twenty-six-year-old German patent clerk Albert Einstein. Here are the four topics and related assertions:

1. the photoelectric effect: light comes in bundles of energy called quanta;
2. atomic dimensions: the size of atoms can be deduced from the analysis of the microscopic "Brownian" motion of small particles suspended in a liquid;
3. special relativity: the speed of light is the same as measured in all rest frames;
4. mass-energy equivalence: mass and energy can change from one to the other.

If Miller and Morley had believed number 3, they would have packed up their interferometer and found other things to study. But not many physicists in 1905 understood Einstein's predictions.

With the arrival in our story of Einstein and his relativity, it is time to update the spelling of the word aether. We shall leave the nineteenth century word behind. *Ether* it shall be.

The ether-drift experiments were originally described as the search for an absolute reference frame. With Einstein's prediction that there is no such thing as an absolute reference frame, these experiments might be better described as attempts to verify or disprove Einstein's relativity. Special relativity requires that lengths of moving objects are contracted, and time intervals measured by moving clocks are dilated. That's the only way to keep the speed of light constant from one rest frame to another. But these predictions were not possible to test since the effects become significant only at very high speeds.[40] In 1905, there was nothing around the lab that could be measured that travels anywhere fast enough. The ether-drift experiments offered the only feasible tests. Relativity predicts zero fringe-shift in the interferometry experiment.

"Special relativity" is *special* because it applies only to relative motions with constant speed in a fixed direction. But there are many other motions in the universe which must be described. Einstein thought about this problem for a decade and, in 1915, proposed "general relativity." This unification of special relativity and Newton's law of gravity extends relativity to any type of motion, including things like the motion of a planet around the sun. We must add a fifth item to the Einstein list:

5. general relativity: the properties of space and time are directly related to the amount of matter and radiation present.

What then was Eddington doing with his telescope on May 29, 1919, on that tropical isle? He was there to test one of the predictions of Einstein's general relativity. According to the theory, light coming from a distant star that passes close to the edge of the sun should be deflected by the sun's gravity.[41] Einstein's calculations predicted that the direction of the starlight would be changed by a tiny angle, two arc-seconds or less (one arc-second is 1/3600 of a degree). Thus, the star would appear to be very slightly displaced from its normal position.

The only way one can see a star whose light passes very close to the sun is during a total eclipse, when the moon blocks the sun's intense light. Einstein had been urging astronomers to look for this effect as early as 1910 and quite a

---

[40] For example, for the measured length of an object which is flying past you to be ten percent less than its length measured when the object is at rest, it must be traveling at four-tenths the speed of light. This shorter length is not some sort of "apparent" length; it is the true length in your rest-frame.

[41] Technically, it is more correct to say that the starlight follows a straight line through space, which is distorted by the sun's gravity.

few had done so by chasing total eclipses or by studying existing photographs. But no one had come up with definitive results; the deflection was just too small. In 1919, Arthur Eddington, head of the Cambridge Observatory, and Frank Dyson, head of the Greenwich Observatory, each set out to observe an upcoming eclipse to test Einstein's theory. The first went to Principe, near the west coast of Africa, the other headed to Sobral, near the northeast coast of Brazil.

Eddington measured the positions of seven different stars which appear very close to the sun. The tiny measured angular displacements, from one to two arc-seconds, strongly supported Einstein's predictions. It was not until the following November that the final analyses were announced at the meeting of the Royal Astronomical Society. *The New York Times* headline: "Einstein Theory Triumphs." Einstein's life changed immediately, from a little-known theoretical physicist living in the turmoil of post-war Berlin to a world celebrity, though few people understood what he had achieved. The *Times* writer admitted (in a statement longing for a few commas): "Efforts made to put in words intelligible to the nonscientific public the Einstein theory of light proved by the eclipse expedition so far have not been very successful." Eddington became the spokesman for Einstein's general relativity in the English-speaking world, most of which was neither aware of nor interested in the German fellow. An interviewer commented to Eddington that there were probably only three people in the world who understood relativity. The astronomer is said to have responded, "Who's the third?"

Before 1919, the famous acoustician and science popularizer, Professor Dayton C. Miller, was certainly better known, at least in America, than Einstein. Miller returned to Cleveland that fall, having presented his report on the sounds of artillery explosions. He surely read in the Cleveland press about Einstein's great success.

In a lecture given in England some years later, Miller said "the deflection of the light from the stars by the sun, as predicted by the theory of relativity, was put to test at the solar eclipse of 1919. The results were widely accepted as confirming the theory. This revived the writer's interest in the ether-drift experiments, the interpretation of which had never been acceptable to him." [42] By "interpretation," he meant "zero fringe shift." He had never believed that that the earlier experiments had proved the *nonexistence* of the ether. More

[42] *The Measurement of Ether Drift*, D. C. Miller Lecture at the Royal Institution, June 1926.

importantly, he had no doubt that those experiments could be improved upon. Miller's "revived" interest would soon lead to action.

By 1919, much had been learned about the universe and the earth's motion through it. The seemingly random motion of stars, small changes in their coordinates on the sky, held a clue to the motion of the sun (along with its little entourage of planets). A statistical study of these motions showed that many stars seemed to be moving preferentially in one direction—an observation that probably meant that our sun and we are moving in the opposite direction. Astronomers, as early as the mid-eighteenth century, had been aware of this proposal and had reported a definite motion of the sun toward the constellation Hercules. If the sun is moving through the ether, then interpretation of any ether-drift experiments must take that into account. Remember, in the ether-drift experiments, emphasis was placed on the *orbital* motion of the earth at 30 kilometers per second. This motion is in one direction in January and in the opposite direction in July as the earth circles the sun. Miller knew in 1919 that things get much more complicated when one includes the effect of the sun's motion through space.

He also knew that a favored explanation for the non-observation of the *full* 30 km/sec drift was ether-drag: the proposal that the earth drags the ether along with it. Both the motion of the solar system and ether-drag must be addressed, that is, *if* one were to repeat the ether-drift experiment.

# Chapter 15 Alone on the Mountain

George Ellery Hale was the director of the Mount Wilson Observatory, located high in the San Gabriel Mountains near Pasadena, California. Hale, a leading American astronomer, was responsible for the construction in 1917 of the 100-inch Hooker telescope. Michelson was one of its earliest users; and in 1919, he fitted it out with an auxiliary optical system and used interferometry to make the first measurement of a star's diameter.[43] The star Betelgeuse turned out to be about as big as our entire solar system! Mount Wilson was at the center of American observational astronomy, and Hale and his colleagues were keenly interested in the role of astronomy in testing Dr. Einstein's relativity.

Hale's own principal interest was the study of the sun. He built a solar observatory and developed a device he called a spectro-heliograph with which he could photograph lines of the solar spectrum. His goal was to understand the environment, composition, and movements of atoms in the chaotic solar atmosphere. Hale was the first to detect the strong magnetic fields associated with storms on the sun that result in sun spots.

From 1915 on, studies of the solar spectrum related to more than just solar weather reports: they could possibly provide a second test of general relativity. In addition to predicting the bending of light passing near the sun, Einstein maintained that light coming from the sun, or even more so, light from a very dense star, would have to fight its way against gravity, losing some of its energy on the way. This would result in a "gravitational redshift," and this too might be looked for by astronomers. Furthermore, Einstein proposed a third

---

[43] Michelson and his collaborator, Francis Pease, were the first to apply this technique. They blocked off the main mirror and placed a twenty-foot-long beam in front of the telescope. The beam carried two narrow slits and mirrors which redirected two pencils of star-light into the telescope where they produced an interference pattern. The spacing of the resulting fringes depended on the tiny angular spread of the light coming from the star, and thus on the star's diameter.

astronomical test of general relativity: the precession of the orbit of Mercury. Planetary astronomers were able to use Newtonian physics to calculate the rate at which the inner planet's orbit shifted with time, but their very precise measurements showed that the calculated rate was too small by a bit less than 1 percent. Einstein asserted that general relativity accounts for this difference.

In summary, there were four ways to test relativity:

1. look for ether-drift;
2. measure the tiny bending of starlight as it passes by the sun;
3. measure the tiny shifts in wavelengths of spectral lines in emissions from dense stars;
4. measure tiny changes in Mercury's orbit.

Many, perhaps most, in the world's physics community in 1920 considered Einstein's relativity to be incomprehensible and counter-intuitive. They expected that the theory would be falsified. For two decades, testing relativity would be the number one challenge. Three of the four tests belonged to the realm of the astronomers, who tackled them with enthusiasm. The earlier ether-drift searches, in the opinion of many, had not been conclusive, either way.

In the spring of 1920, Miller contacted Hale with a proposal that he should come out to Mount Wilson and give the ether-drift experiment another try, this time at an elevation of 5700 feet.[44] Surely that would reduce ether-drag—if there were such a thing. Hale had in fact been discussing a possible repetition of the experiment with both Michelson and the eighty-two-year-old Morley. Although each had serious doubts about the claims of a 6 to 10-kilometer-per-second drift, they agreed that it was worth another try. So in the summer of 1920, Hale wrote to Miller inviting him to set up his interferometer at the Mount Wilson complex.

Mount Wilson was not just a "higher hill"; it was the place where the "action" was, where physics and astronomy were coming together to achieve a better understanding of the universe. Hale was determined to create a vital center for cutting-edge research at Pasadena, Caltech, and Mount Wilson. He lured Robert Millikan from the University of Chicago to take over as president

---

[44] This exchange of letters is preserved among the G. E. Hale papers at the Archives of the American Institute of Physics, courtesy Roberto Lalli of the University of Milan.

of Caltech. (Millikan would later be awarded a Nobel Prize for measuring the electron's charge.)

In August, Miller and his wife took the train out to Oakland, California, on a previously planned trip to spend three weeks with his siblings and their families. They had left the family home in Ohio years earlier. Miller took advantage of his visit to the Bay Area to give a lecture at the University of California, Berkeley, describing his Sandy Hook artillery work. He then traveled south, on September 10, to visit Mount Wilson and to meet with Michelson, Hale, and Hale's new young assistant, Edwin Hubble. They drove the ten miles up the breathtaking twists of the Mount Wilson Toll Road to check out the site proposed for a new ether-drift laboratory. Returning to Cleveland, Miller had to look into the logistics of moving the equipment and to identify sources of funds.

**The road up Mount Wilson**

The steel-based interferometer was shipped to California; and in March of 1921, Miller arrived to set it up. He was accompanied by his former Case student and invaluable assistant, Ralph Hovey. Hovey had been Miller's right-hand man for over a decade in the sound analysis work. Another traveling companion was CSAS treasurer, Eckstein Case, who clearly had some financial interest in the endeavor. Eventually, Miller would receive additional funding from the Carnegie Institution for Science, which provided the funds for essentially all of the Mount Wilson Observatory. Not one to miss an opportunity to give a public lecture, Miller entertained audiences with his phonodeik sound demonstrations at Caltech, UCLA, and USC.

Within the month, the interferometer was installed on concrete piers in a tar paper and canvas tent, and Miller began accumulating data. Once again there were signs of an ether-drift, indicating an earth-ether relative speed of about 10 km/sec, but Miller decided that the setup had to be improved before making any public announcement. (Remember, extraneous effects of one part in a hundred million would invalidate the experiment.) To eliminate possible magnetostriction caused by motion of the interferometer through the earth's magnetic field, the steel base was replaced by one made of concrete reinforced with brass. The steel base eventually proved to be more reliable and was restored for subsequent runs. In addition, construction of a new and more substantial enclosure was begun at another location on Mount Wilson, one better protected from wind and weather.

**"Ether-house" on Mount Wilson**

In May, Miller returned to Cleveland to close out the semester and participate in the 1921 graduation ceremonies. On that very weekend, Miller welcomed a surprise visitor, someone who had come to Case expressly to meet him and to discuss his work. His guest book, now part of the Library of Congress D. C. Miller Collection, contained one line in small, neat handwriting: "Albert Einstein Berlin (Haberlandstr. 5) 25 Mai 21." The world-famous theorist was travelling with Chaim Weizmann, the future president of Israel, on a tour to raise money for the establishment of an independent Zionist state of Israel. At their meeting in Miller's Rockefeller Hall, Einstein expressed admiration for the great effort Miller was putting into getting unambiguous results from the ether-drift experiment. It was in Einstein's interest for someone, somewhere, to get the experiment done properly and presumably put an end to the ether idea once and for all. For starters, data should be collected at different times of the year. Miller's German was excellent, thanks to his undergraduate studies at the Baldwin school and the two men spent an interesting afternoon together.

**Einstein signs Miller's guest book (line 6)**

Einstein, being a polite and diplomatic gentleman, probably did not repeat to Miller, that day, a remark which he had made at Princeton a few days earlier. Having been informed that Miller was continuing to claim a non-zero ether effect, the father of relativity made what has become a frequently quoted observation: *Raffiniert ist der Herr Gott, aber boshaft ist Er nicht.* Subtle is the Lord, but malicious He is not.

California was too far away, and the facilities on the mountaintop too primitive for any systematic search for improvements that might be made. Besides, Miller did have a full-time commitment to his duties as chairman of the Case physics department. By the end of 1921, he decided to ship everything back to Cleveland. For a full two years, he worked on optimizing every aspect of the experiment, working conveniently and comfortably in his first-floor lab in the Rockefeller building. He tried arc lights, automobile headlights, sunlight, and other light sources. He experimented with different telescopes and mirrors. He tried photographing the fringes. He used electrical heaters in a systematic study of temperature effects. He replaced the moving telescope with a simple eyepiece attached to a moving arm and a large objective lens fixed to the center of the interferometer. This magnified the fringes by a factor of fifty "so that direct reading with the eye was very satisfactory." [45]

In April, 1922, Miller, recently elected to the National Academy of Sciences, received a second distinguished visitor at Case. This time it was the 1902 Nobel Laureate, Hendrik A. Lorentz, who had for thirty years been at the center of the ether-relativity debate. He was on his way back to the Netherlands after spending two months lecturing at Caltech as a guest of Hale. (Miller's guest book entry: H. A. Lorentz Haarlem, Netherlands April 5, 1922, and a note in Miller's hand "Lectured in my Lecture Room, Case and WRU auspices. 400 present.") Lorentz was keenly supportive of what Miller was trying to do at Mount Wilson. It has been reported that when Miller invited Lorentz to take a look at the fringes in his interferometer, the famous theorist confessed that he had never before seen white-light optical interference patterns. That makes three Nobel laureates (Michelson, Einstein, and Lorentz) who, each for his own reasons, encouraged Miller to persevere!

**Interferometer set up at Case in 1922**

45 Quotation from the "final" Miller paper: The Ether-Drift Experiment and the Determination of the Absolute Motion of the Earth" *Reviews of Modern Physics* **5** 203-242 (1933).

Miller welcomes H. A. Lorentz to Case

# MAY DETHRONE EINSTEIN

## *Dr. Miller of Case to Launch New Attack*

### Prepares 6-Month Test to Prove Ether Drift Exists.

**By William Dinwoodie.**

PROFESSOR DAYTON C. MILLER, noted physicist of Case School of Applied Science, is preparing to knock Professor Einstein and his relativity theory into a cocked hat.

Dr. Miller didn't put it in quite those words when he announced his future plans today but his friends are certain he won't be satisfied with less than Dr. Einstein's scalp when it is all over.

The argument centers around the possible presence of an ether drift in the space beyond this rather small world.

From previous experiments, Dr. Miller has become convinced that there is such a drift. Dr. Einstein has been inclined to pooh-pooh the suggestion.

He refused to acknowledge the drift in making his relativity calculations that astounded scientists throughout the world.

* * *

NOW, if Dr. Miller conclusively proves the presence of the drift it will be sure to prove a sad blow to Dr. Einstein for it will mean that he will have to discard his old theory and start all over again.

That the Case scientist is preparing for a final showdown is indicated by the extent of his plans.

Sensationalist press coverage

# Chapter 16 Perseverance

Relativity was far from being fully accepted. The literature was full of counter-claims, many of which clung firmly to the ether. Einstein was awarded the 1921 Nobel Prize in Physics for his work on the photoelectric effect—not relativity. The literature, popular and technical, was full of refutations of Einstein's claims.[46]

The search for the ether and the testing of relativity were not the only things going on at Mount Wilson in 1922. As a result of observations made there by Edwin Hubble, the estimated size of the universe had swollen a hundred-billion-fold.[47]

In Cleveland, Miller continued work on refining the ether-drift experiment until the summer of 1924, when he once again packed everything up and set out for Mount Wilson. Around this time, Walter S. Adams, a longtime assistant of Hale, was appointed as the new director of the observatory. Miller would need Adams's respect and support in continuing his measurements at Mount Wilson.

In his "summary" publication a full decade later, Miller describes his thinking at the time: "It was felt that if any of the suspected disturbing causes

---

46 Among these was a book "*Gravitation versus Relativity*" by Columbia University professor of celestial mechanics, Charles Lane Poor. We met Poor before. He was the Johns Hopkins graduate student who shared Lexell's comet with Miller back in 1889.

47 Hubble was able to determine the distances to those fuzzy objects called nebulae, which were thought to be clouds of gas in our Milky Way galaxy. He used a technique discovered in 1908 which depended on "Cepheid Variables." These stars vary in brightness at a rate which is correlated with their intrinsic brightness. One can use the observed rate of variation along with the observed brightness to determine the actual distance to the star. This "measuring stick" eventually revolutionized the astronomers' picture of the universe, when Hubble showed that the nebulae were enormously distant galaxies and that our Milky Way galaxy is just one among billions.

had been responsible for the previously observed effects, now these were removed, the result would be a true null effect. Such a conclusion would have been accepted with entire satisfaction; and indeed it was almost expected. On the other hand, if the observations continued to give the positive effect, it would certainly have to be considered as real." One might reasonably add: if the observations continued to give a definite positive effect, a Nobel Prize would be a sure thing.

In August of 1924, with Adams's approval, the improved interferometer was installed in the new observing hut, away from any windy canyon edges. Special attention was paid to temperature stability. New measurements were begun, as Miller wrote, "in a wholly unprejudiced but very confident state of mind." Presumably all the potential bugs had been worked out, and it was time to collect data. But how much data would be enough? All the earlier experiments sought evidence specifically for the 30 km/sec orbital motion of the earth through the ether. If everything were working perfectly, Michelson and Morley in 1887 could simply point their telescope in the direction of the earth's orbital motion and turn the sandstone block *a single quarter turn*, and they would see a shift of four-tenths of a fringe; and *voilá*, the experiment is finished, the ether is verified, and relativity is in trouble.

Miller described a more general objective: he will search for *any* movement of the interferometer through the ether at all times of the day and all seasons of the year. That should allow one to determine the rotational and orbital components and then to extract the constant velocity of the solar system through space. This was more difficult than it might sound because the interferometer samples only the light beams lying in the optical plane of its two arms. Miller built mechanical models made of spheres and rods and disks to help him visualize this complicated combination of motions. The computation would be even harder than the cometary orbit calculations he had made thirty-five years earlier as a Princeton graduate student.

Data-taking began in September of 1924 and was continued in April, August, and September of 1925 and February of 1926. The total involved over twelve thousand turns of the interferometer. Now, for the first time, data were systematically collected for all "seasons," that is, for each quadrant of the earth's orbit. Remember, Michelson and Morley never got around to doing this, and the Miller-Morley attempts yielded no information on "directional" effects.

Partway through the data-taking (in April of 1925), APS President Miller spoke at a meeting of the National Academy of Sciences in Washington. He felt confident enough in the analyses to that point to announce a definite 10 km/sec relative motion and to promise that the data would soon provide information on the motion of the solar system. The following December, at the meeting of the AAAS in Kansas City, Miller went further, announcing motion of the solar system toward the constellation Draco at 200 km/sec. His detailed presentation was very convincing: Miller was awarded the AAAS Newcomb Prize of one thousand dollars for the best paper at the meeting. Some authors have suggested that the selection of Miller was pushed by the "anti-relativity forces."

Some of Einstein's thinking about Miller and his work appear in a 1925 letter to well-known editor, writer, and respected popularizer of science, Edwin Slosson. "My opinion about Miller's experiments is the following . . . Should the positive result be confirmed, then the special theory of relativity and with it the general theory of relativity, in its current form, would be invalid. *Experimentum summus judex*." (Experiment is the highest judge.)

Some of Miller's thinking about Einstein and the origins of relativity appears in a 1926 paper in *Science*. After describing his 1905 work with Morley, he writes: "It was at this time that Einstein became interested; and in November, 1905, he published a paper on 'The Electrodynamics of Moving Bodies' . . . The whole theory was related to physical phenomena, largely on the assumption that the ether-drift experiments of Michelson, Morley, and Miller had given a definite and exact null result."[48] The figure below is from one of the lantern slides which Miller used to state his case. It shows how the "arch of Einstein" rests first on the three astronomical tests but ultimately on the Michelson-Morley experiment.[49] We shall describe Einstein's take on this erroneous claim in the "Epilogues" at the end of this book.

---

48 *Science* **43** 433-443 (1926).

49 This dubious interpretation persists to this day, when the first chapter of typical "modern physics" textbooks jumps from the Michelson-Morley experiment directly to special relativity.

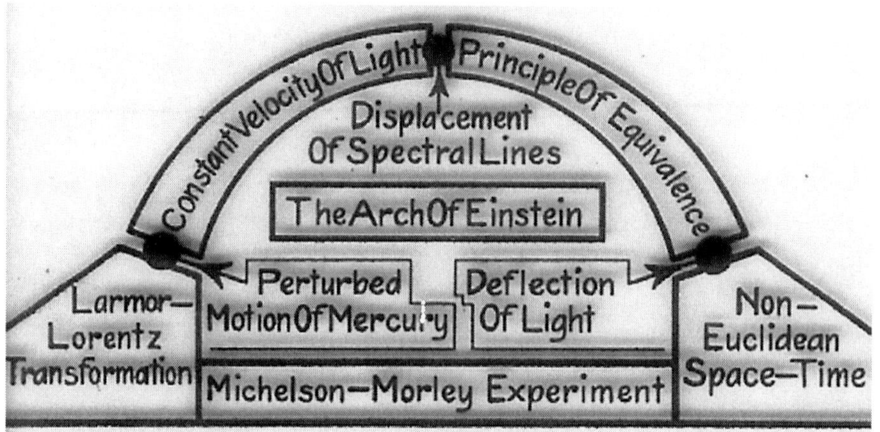


**The arch of Einstein**

What do Miller's new data look like? For the entire series of observations (September, 1924 to February, 1926), the data were recorded in the same format. The time, date, temperature, and general weather conditions were noted on each paper chart. As the observer moved the stone along, an electric bell sounded every 22.5 degrees, that is, sixteen gongs for the full circle. With his eye to the telescope, he quickly called out his estimate (in units of one-tenth of a fringe) of the position of the central fringe relative to the vertical crosshair. His assistant recorded those sixteen numbers per turn. A typical run involved twenty turns. The twenty readings for each angle are averaged and then plotted on graph paper, fringe displacement versus angle. In the "idealized experiment" (perfect alignment with the earth's orbit, no experimental defects, and a full 30 km/sec drift), each plot of sixteen points should look like a perfect double-humped sine wave with amplitude of about half a fringe. The typical plots were far from being so smooth and had typical amplitudes more like one-seventh of a fringe.

**Miller adjusts mirrors at Mount Wilson.**

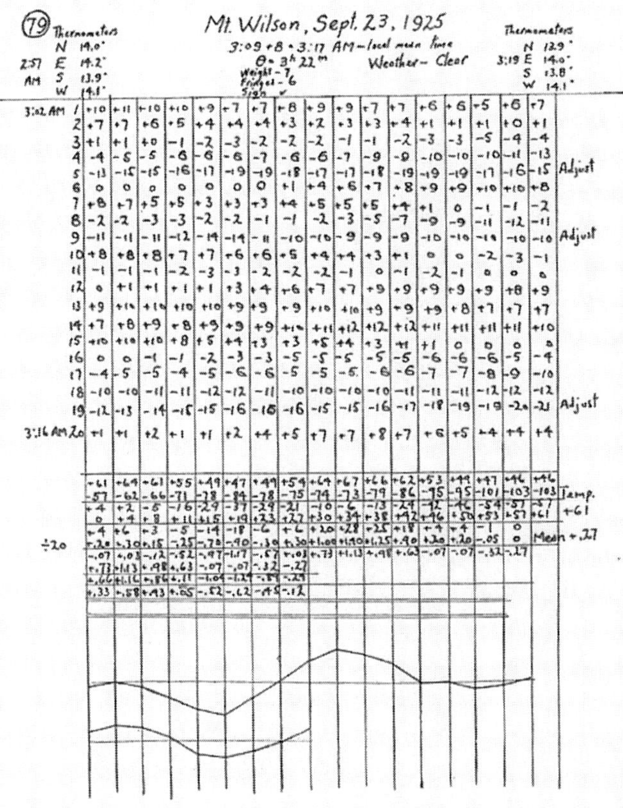

(79) Mt. Wilson, Sept. 23, 1925

Thermometers: 2:57 AM — N 14.0° E 14.2° S 13.9° W 14.1°

3:09 + 8 = 3:17 AM – local mean time
θ = 3h 22m  Weather – Clear
Weight – 7
Fringes – 6
Sign ✓

Thermometers: 3:19 — N 12.9° E 14.0° S 13.8° W 14.1°

| | | | | | | | | | | | | | | | | | | | |
|---|---|---|---|---|---|---|---|---|---|---|---|---|---|---|---|---|---|---|---|
| 3:02 AM | 1 | +10 | +11 | +10 | +10 | +9 | +7 | +7 | +8 | +9 | +9 | +7 | +7 | +6 | +6 | +5 | +6 | +7 | |
| | 2 | +7 | +7 | +6 | +5 | +4 | +4 | +4 | +3 | +2 | +3 | +3 | +4 | +1 | +1 | +1 | +0 | +1 | |
| | 3 | +1 | +1 | +0 | -1 | -2 | -3 | -2 | -2 | -2 | -1 | -1 | -2 | -3 | -3 | -5 | -4 | -4 | |
| | 4 | -4 | -5 | -5 | -6 | -6 | -6 | -7 | -6 | -6 | -7 | -9 | -9 | -10 | -10 | -10 | -11 | -13 | |
| | 5 | -13 | -15 | -15 | -16 | -17 | -19 | -19 | -18 | -17 | -17 | -18 | -19 | -19 | -19 | -17 | -16 | -15 | Adjust |
| | 6 | 0 | 0 | 0 | 0 | 0 | 0 | 0 | +1 | +4 | +6 | +7 | +8 | +9 | +9 | +10 | +10 | +8 | |
| | 7 | +8 | +7 | +5 | +5 | +3 | +3 | +3 | +4 | +5 | +5 | +5 | +4 | +1 | 0 | -1 | -1 | -2 | |
| | 8 | -2 | -2 | -3 | -3 | -2 | -2 | -1 | -1 | -2 | -3 | -5 | -7 | -9 | -9 | -11 | -12 | -11 | |
| | 9 | -11 | -11 | -11 | -12 | -14 | -14 | -11 | -10 | -10 | -9 | -9 | -9 | -10 | -10 | -10 | -10 | -10 | Adjust |
| | 10 | +8 | +8 | +8 | +7 | +7 | +6 | +6 | +5 | +4 | +4 | +3 | +1 | 0 | 0 | -2 | -3 | -1 | |
| | 11 | -1 | -1 | -1 | -2 | -3 | -3 | -2 | -2 | -2 | -1 | 0 | -1 | -2 | -1 | 0 | 0 | 0 | |
| | 12 | 0 | +1 | +1 | +1 | +1 | +3 | +4 | +6 | +7 | +7 | +9 | +9 | +9 | +9 | +9 | +8 | +9 | |
| | 13 | +9 | +10 | +10 | +10 | +10 | +9 | +9 | +9 | +10 | +10 | +9 | +9 | +9 | +8 | +7 | +7 | +7 | |
| | 14 | +7 | +8 | +9 | +8 | +9 | +9 | +9 | +10 | +11 | +12 | +12 | +12 | +11 | +11 | +11 | +11 | +10 | |
| | 15 | +10 | +10 | +10 | +8 | +5 | +4 | +3 | +3 | +5 | +4 | +3 | +1 | +1 | 0 | 0 | 0 | 0 | |
| | 16 | 0 | 0 | -1 | -1 | -2 | -3 | -3 | -5 | -5 | -5 | -5 | -5 | -6 | -6 | -6 | -5 | -4 | |
| | 17 | -4 | -5 | -5 | -4 | -5 | -6 | -6 | -5 | -5 | -6 | -6 | -6 | -7 | -7 | -8 | -9 | -10 | |
| | 18 | -10 | -10 | -11 | -11 | -12 | -12 | -11 | -10 | -10 | -10 | -10 | -11 | -11 | -11 | -12 | -12 | -12 | |
| | 19 | -12 | -13 | -14 | -15 | -15 | -16 | -16 | -16 | -15 | -15 | -16 | -17 | -18 | -19 | -19 | -20 | -21 | Adjust |
| 3:16 AM | 20 | +1 | +1 | +2 | +1 | +1 | +2 | +4 | +5 | +7 | +7 | +8 | +7 | +6 | +5 | +4 | +4 | +4 | |
| | | +61 | +64 | +61 | +55 | +49 | +47 | +49 | +54 | +64 | +67 | +66 | +62 | +53 | +49 | +47 | +46 | +46 | |
| | | -57 | -62 | -66 | -71 | -78 | -84 | -78 | -75 | -74 | -73 | -79 | -86 | -95 | -95 | -101 | -103 | -103 | Temp. |
| | | +4 | +2 | -5 | -16 | -29 | -37 | -29 | -21 | -10 | -6 | -13 | -24 | -42 | -46 | -54 | -57 | -57 | +61 |
| | | 0 | +4 | +8 | +11 | +15 | +19 | +23 | +27 | +30 | +34 | +38 | +42 | +46 | +50 | +53 | +57 | +61 | |
| | | +4 | +6 | +3 | -5 | -14 | -18 | -6 | +6 | +20 | +28 | +25 | +18 | +4 | +4 | -1 | 0 | | Mean +.27 |
| ÷20 | | +.20 | +.30 | +.15 | -.25 | -.70 | -.90 | -.30 | +.30 | +1.00 | +1.40 | +1.25 | +.90 | +.20 | +.20 | -.05 | 0 | | |
| | | -.07 | +.03 | -.12 | -.52 | -.97 | -1.17 | -.57 | +.03 | +.73 | +1.13 | +.98 | +.63 | -.07 | -.07 | -.32 | -.27 | | |
| | | +.73 | +1.13 | +.98 | +.63 | -.07 | -.07 | -.32 | -.27 | | | | | | | | | | |
| | | +.66 | +1.16 | +.86 | +.11 | -1.04 | -1.24 | -.89 | -.24 | | | | | | | | | | |
| | | +.33 | +.58 | +.43 | +.05 | -.52 | -.62 | -.45 | -.12 | | | | | | | | | | |

**Sample raw-data page**

Miller accumulated hundreds of plots like this. The challenge was to extract the size of any true signal, as a function of time and date. A few chapters ago we described how Miller analyzed the sounds of musical instruments and spoken vowels. He would take a waveform produced by his phonodeik, plot it on paper, and trace it with the pointer of his wonderful Henrici harmonic analyzer. The little counters on the machine registered the amplitudes and phases of each harmonic component. This is just what was needed for the ether-drift data! In principle, a true fringe shift would show up in the second harmonic amplitude and phase. Noise and instrumental errors would be herded into the other harmonics. That's only the beginning. In order to make sense of the results, the size *and* phase of any fringe shift must be tracked through the day and through the year, as the light paths in the plane of the interferometer point in constantly changing directions.

Miller and his faithful assistant Hovey, along with Case physics students, spent many long hours plotting the data and running it through the Henrici.[50] The analyses of the interferometer data continued for several years. Miller, along with many others in the physics world, had no doubt that the ether would eventually show itself. Meanwhile, the public was interested in anything associated with Einstein and his exotic theory. A *New York Times* article about Miller in 1925 announced "Strikes a Blow against Relativity." The following year, the *Cleveland Plain Dealer* featured the city's number-one physicist's role in a lead article. The headline: "Goes to Disprove Einstein's Theory. Case Scientist Will Conduct Further Studies in Ether-drift—Einstein Discounts Experiments." The article quotes Miller: "The trouble with Prof. Einstein is that he knows nothing about my results; he has been saying for thirty years that the interferometer experiments in Cleveland showed negative results. We never said they gave negative results, and they did not in fact give negative results. He ought to give me credit for knowing that temperature differences would affect the results. He wrote to me in November suggesting this. I am not so simple as to make no allowance for temperature."[51]

---

50 One of his brightest students was Philip Morse, a junior physics major in 1924, who worked long hard hours on the project. Morse went on to earn a PhD at Princeton and to become a world-famous physicist on the faculty of MIT. In his 1977 autobiography, Morse described Miller as "tiny and neat and polished, with an imposing moustache, beautiful white, wavy hair, and a pleasant but very formal manner. His lectures were clear but not theatrical; his lecture demonstrations were carefully planned and always worked."

51 Einstein was very much aware of the impact of Miller's claims on the physics community. In a 1926 newspaper article titled "My Theory and Miller's Research,"

# Chapter 17 Diminishing Indications

The question of whether Miller was really seeing an ether-drift or whether Einstein's prediction of no drift prevailed was argued across the physics community. In February of 1927, a conference was held at the Mount Wilson Observatory to assess the situation. The conference proceedings begin: "The presence of Professor A. A. Michelson and Professor H. A. Lorentz in Pasadena in the early months of 1927 offered an exceptional opportunity for a conference on the theoretical and practical aspects of the Michelson-Morley experiment."

Michelson spoke first. He gave a two-minute summary of his famous work with Morley forty years earlier. "The shift of fringes was certainly less than 1/20 and maybe even 1/40 of that predicted by the theory. The result could be accounted for by the assumption that the earth drags the ether along nearly at its full speed . . ." Michelson continued, "Lorentz then suggested another explanation," (Lorentz contraction), "which in its final form yielded as a result the famous Lorentz transformations. These contain the gist of the whole relativity theory." (Einstein, if he were there, would have been bemused by that rather simplified attribution.) Michelson went on: "The Michelson-Morley experiment was continued by Morley and Miller, who again obtained a negative result.

---

he wrote: "If the results of the Miller experiments were to be confirmed, then relativity theory could not be maintained, since the experiments would then prove that, relative to the coordinate systems of the appropriate state of motion (the Earth), the velocity of light in a vacuum would depend upon the direction of motion. With this, the principle of the constancy of the velocity of light, which forms one of the two foundation pillars on which the theory is based, would be refuted." Translation in "*Einstein's Attitude Towards Experiments*," Klaus Hentschel, *Stud. Hist. Phil. Sci.* **23** 593 (1992). Courtesy Roberto Lalli. Lalli is completing research for a history of science doctorate at the University of Milan. He has analyzed an extensive collection of articles and correspondence by key players on both sides of the 1920-1930 ether debate. Publication of his work is expected in 2011.

Miller then continued alone, and seems now to get some positive effect. This effect, however, has nothing to do with the orbital motion of the earth. It seems to be due to a velocity of the solar system relative to stellar space, which may be much greater than the orbital velocity. The observations of Mr. Miller have stimulated new interest in the problem."[52]

Michelson was nowhere near giving up on the ether. In his book on optics published that same year, he wrote that while the theory of relativity "must be accorded a generous acceptance, the existence of an ether appears to be inconsistent with the theory . . . But without a medium how can the propagation of light waves be explained? How explain the constancy of propagation, the fundamental assumption if there be no medium?"

The second speaker was Lorentz. Probably in response to Michelson's comment, Lorentz declared: "The theory of relativity is really solely Einstein's work. And there can be no doubt that he would have conceived it even if the work of all his predecessors in the theory of this field had not been done at all. His work is in this respect independent of the previous theories." Lorentz concluded that the absence of the expected fringe displacement in the Michelson-Morley experiment "is accounted for by the well-known contraction hypothesis. Asked if I consider this contraction as a real one, I should answer yes. It is as real as anything that we can observe."

It was then Dayton Miller's turn. With the experience he had gained from the hundreds of lectures given over the preceding thirty years, Miller presented a complete and clear, though rather lengthy, summary of the work to date. He described first the Michelson-Morley 1887 results and then how Lord Kelvin had urged Morley and him to give it another try when they met at the Paris Congress in 1900. He stated that the subsequent 1902-'05 measurements "give a definite positive effect of about one tenth of the then-expected result."

In a smooth transition to his more recent work, Miller began by repeating the statement we quoted earlier: "The deflection of the light from the stars by the sun, as predicted by the theory of relativity, was put to test at the solar eclipse of 1919. The results were widely accepted as confirming the theory. This revived the writer's interest in the ether-drift experiments, the interpretation of which had never been acceptable to him." He then went on to describe all the painstaking work done in Cleveland and Mount Wilson from 1921 to 1925. "I think I am not egotistical but am merely stating a fact when it is remarked that the ether-drift observations are the most trying and fatiguing, as regards

[52] Conference on the Michelson-Morley Experiment, held at Mount Wilson Observatory, *Astrophysical Journal* 68 (1928).

physical, mental, and nervous strain, of any scientific work with which I am acquainted." Doubters of the validity of his claims would, in later years, refer to this remark on the experimental difficulties of the technique.

Miller pointed out that all the previous attempts were directed at detecting the effects of particular motions of the interferometer through the ether: the daily rotation, the yearly revolution, the proposed linear motion of the solar system, or as yet unknown motions of the galaxy. Forget about all these components, he said, and simply compile data at many times of the day and the year and look for *any* systematic fringe-shift patterns, whatever their source. *Any* demonstrable variation of *any* size in the speed of light would be sufficient to prove the existence of the ether.

In this spirit, what then do all the data show? Miller was convinced that his entire data set was consistent with an ether-drift of about 10 km/sec, only one third of the speed of the earth's orbital motion. That could be the result of the ether being dragged along by the earth. However, since comparable fringe shifts were seen in Cleveland and on the heights of Mount Wilson, any ether-drag is not reduced at higher altitudes. What one saw seemed likely to be related to the motion of the solar system. He ended his talk by acknowledging that the results were less than unambiguous and promising that the analysis would be continued in Cleveland.

Three more speakers followed Miller. Roy Kennedy of Caltech described a mini-version of an interferometer experiment which included some clever optical improvements.[53] He claimed that no drift greater than ~3 km/s was observed, either at the campus lab in Pasadena or in the 100-inch-telescope building up on Mount Wilson. E. R. Hedrick of UCLA presented a very complicated analysis of the fringe-shift technique in general, concluding that, in his opinion, the process of averaging multiple observations was inappropriate. And finally, Paul Epstein of Caltech gave a brief review of three other ether-drift searches, two involving the torque on a magnetic needle located near a charged condenser, the third a standard interferometer experiment performed at 2300 meters above Brussels in a balloon-borne gondola lab. None of these attempts indicated an ether-drift. Epstein concludes, however: "Although interesting, these experiments cannot therefore decide either for or against Miller's results. On this account it would be of great value if they could be carried out with increased precision."

---

53 It is interesting that Miller stressed the importance of using a long light path to produce a large fringe shift while Kennedy argued that a shorter light path would allow better mechanical and temperature control. R. J. Kennedy, *Publications of the National Academy of Sciences* **12** 621 (1926).

Then the "discussion session" began, with Lorentz and Michelson commenting on Miller's results, both of them agreeing that more work was needed to understand them. Astronomer Gustaf Strömberg of the Mount Wilson Observatory, an expert on stellar motions, brought the discussion up to date by pointing out that recent discoveries showed that the universe is much larger than formerly believed. While the sun may move at 20 km/sec relative to nearby bright stars, its speed relative to distant globular star clusters is more like 300 km/sec, "and relative to the spiral nebulae it may be even larger." That just adds to the difficulty of interpreting Miller's or any other experimental data.

We described earlier how Miller and several of his students used the Henrici mechanical analyzer to search for a regular sinusoidal signal in the interferometer fringe shift data. We identified one of those students, Philip Morse. Miller's evidence for the existence of the ether was based entirely on those analyses. When the separate question of the motion of the solar system came up, Miller and Case astronomy chairman, Jason Nassau, realized that it might be possible to use the Henrici to analyze the observed stellar motions, relative to the solar system, of a large number of stars and to deduce the direction and speed of the sun's motion. This would bring up to date earlier studies of stellar motions. In the summer of 1926, following his graduation, young Morse worked with Professor Nassau, using the Henrici to look for systematic effects in the motions of some five hundred stars. They published a paper in the *Astrophysical Journal* in 1927, concluding that their results for the direction and speed of the sun were in good agreement with Miller's ether-drift results.[54] This provided one more argument for Miller's claims.

Another important and well-reported physics conference took place in Brussels eight months later: the famous 1927 Solvay Conference on Electrons and Photons. It was attended by twenty-nine European physicists, with not one American participating. The list of participants reads like the chapter headings in a history of modern physics. The main discussion involved the meaning of the new quantum theory, with Einstein and Niels Bohr arguing about whether or not "God plays dice." The emphasis had clearly turned from relativity versus ether to particle versus wave.

Nevertheless, the question of the ether's existence remained important enough for other players in the U.S. and Europe to invest a great deal of time and money to find the answer. Michelson, Pease, Kennedy, and others at Mount Wilson built more sophisticated interferometers and saw no ether-drift.

---

[54] P. M. Morse and J.J.Nassau, *The Astrophysical Journal* **65** 73 (1927).

Returning to Chicago, Michelson, and Gale built an enormous interference experiment, an experiment based on what is called the Sagnac effect. The related theory predicts that light directed by mirrors around a closed path while the path itself is rotating, takes longer to complete the trip when travelling in the direction of the rotational motion than light traveling in the opposite direction. Simply put, the mirrors are running away from the former beam and its trip is longer. The Chicago team built a rectangular evacuated tube 2000 feet by 1000 feet and placed it side by side with a second smaller rectangular tube. Light beams travelled in both directions around each rectangle, recombining to form two separate interference patterns. Where does the rotational motion required by the Sagnac effect come in? The two rectangles sit on the rotating earth! The predicted Sagnac fringe shift is proportional to the *area* of the rectangle and the rate of rotation of the earth. (Picture doing the experiment at the North Pole, with the earth turning beneath you.) The observed *difference* between the fringe shift in the large rectangle and that in the small rectangle agreed with the theoretical prediction to within 2 percent. Unfortunately, this result, though gratifying, does not depend on the existence of the ether. Michelson later admitted that all they had shown was that the earth turns.

Another experiment that involves the earth's rotation is that named for Lorand Eötvös. This Hungarian physicist, as early as the 1880s, had devised a way to compare a body's gravitational mass with its inertial mass. The equivalence of these two is central to general relativity. (The Eötvös experiment has nothing to do with the interferometry experiments we have been discussing, but we shall see that it does enter the relativity-test story.) Two objects of different materials are attached to the ends of a horizontal rod, which in turn hangs from a string. Each object feels the downward pull of gravity on its "gravitational mass" and the centrifugal force associated with the rotating earth on its "inertial mass." If these two types of mass are not identical, as required by relativity, then the net forces acting on the two objects will not be parallel to one another, and the suspension string will twist. Some theorists had in fact proposed that a portion of the inertial mass might not feel gravity. Eötvös was able to demonstrate the equivalence of the inertial and gravitational masses with astonishing precision.[55]

In the 1920s, some antirelativists hoped that the Eötvös technique would ultimately disprove general relativity. One of these researchers was another

---

55 Similar Eötvös experiments are still being done today in million-dollar tests of general relativity. The program at Washington University, St. Louis, is named *Eotwash*.

Clevelander, as famous as Dayton Miller, but much wealthier. Charles F. Brush had been a close friend and supporter of Edward Morley as early at 1883. He was the inventor of the arc-light, and his company, Brush Electric, was a leading manufacturer of electric generators. After his company was sold to General Electric, Brush continued to experiment in his basement laboratory on challenging physics topics, including gravity. In 1926, the seventy-seven-year-old Brush wrote to Miller as follows: "Dear Doctor Miller: Of course you know all about the Eotvos Experiment, on which the Relativists pin their faith and which I know to be fallacious in its results . . . Presumably the several experimenters who have tried out the Eotvos method of late years have done so to vindicate their belief in Einstein . . . It has recently occurred to me that if the spirit moves you, and you can spare the time while you are at Mt. Wilson, you can with very little trouble try out the Eotvos Experiment under ideal mechanical conditions by mounting the torsion balance and observing telescope and scale on one arm of your ether-drift apparatus." Miller responded that he would look into the possibility but needed first to learn more about what the experiment would entail. There is no evidence that he went further than that, but the invitation from Brush is an example of the efforts of the anti-relativists.

On the other side, many of the new searches for the ether-drift were championed by *supporters* of relativity who were determined to use the latest technologies to get an unambiguous answer. European physicists Piccard and Stahel continued their balloon flights. By 1930, the German Georg Joos could report results from the greatly improved interferometer built at the famous Zeiss optical works in Jena. Among this growing list of ever more sophisticated and enhanced experiments, Miller's result stood pretty much alone in claiming a significant effect. Furthermore, the size and direction of Miller's ether-drift were not at all understood.

There were other efforts supported by *antirelativists* with a variety of motives. For example, at one extreme was the Hungarian-German physicist and 1905 Nobel laureate, Phillip Lenard, who pressed for replication of the experiment at high altitudes. Lenard was an outspoken supporter of Hitler and an anti-Semite, and he was determined to prove Einstein wrong. A related observation was made by the young Austrian and future Nobelist, Erwin Schrödinger. In a 1925 letter to Wilhelm Wien, Schrödinger wrote: "The result of the Miller experiment is very important but it has been played down in

Jewish circles of physicists. I should like to see the experiment repeated on the Jungfraujoch."[56]

In October, 1929, Miller took part in another conference related to the experimental status of relativity theory. This was part of the annual meeting of the Optical Society of America, held at Cornell University. In his 2006 book, Jeffrey Crelinsten describes this meeting under the title "Antirelativists Rally in the East."[57] Each type of experiment or observation that supported relativity was called into question. Columbia's astronomer Charles Lane Poor questioned the measurements of the bending of stellar light by the sun. Keivin Burns of the University of Pittsburgh did the same about solar redshift measurements. Herbert Morgan of the U.S. Naval Observatory challenged the Mercury perihelion results. William Meggers of the Bureau of Standards disagreed with published stellar redshift data. And to top it off, Dayton Miller argued for the reality of his interferometer fringe shift. As Crelinsten notes, "Every presentation attempted to show that relativity had not been verified."

The following April, the "west coast relativists" dominated a meeting of the National Academy of Sciences, responding clearly and authoritatively to the skeptics in the east. They addressed each of the main points made at the Optical Society Cornell meeting. One of their arguments was that Miller's interferometer was insufficiently reliable to quantify any ether-drift. In this regard, Charles St. John of the Mount Wilson Observatory even quoted Miller's frequent remarks about how difficult it was to make the observations. Later, St. John would contrast Miller's relatively primitive equipment with the vastly improved mechanical and optical components of the Michelson, Pease, and Pearson experiment at Mount Wilson and that of Georg Joos at Jena.

Mount Wilson director Adams sought to end the controversy by asking Michelson, in 1930, to publish a comprehensive report on his interferometry work with Pease and Pearson. Specifically, Adams hoped that the publication of a paper, more detailed than the Michelson *et al.* 1929 account published in *Science*, would settle the issue.[58]

---

56 Quoted in *A Life of Erwin Schrödinger*, Walter Moore, Cambridge University Press, 1994.

57 *Einstein's Jury, the Race to Test Relativity*, Jeffrey Crelinsten, Princeton University Press, 2006. This recent publication provides an excellent and detailed description of the relativity debate.

58 Adams expressed his impatience in a letter to Michelson, writing, "In view of Dayton Miller's rather exasperating statements on this subject, I should like to see your work published in sufficient detail to cut the ground from under him." Courtesy of Roberto Lalli.

Miller had no choice but to press on with the analysis of his data, searching not simply for an ether-drift signal but for *any* effects which might mimic such a signal. One argument he continued to make, concerning the failure of competing experiments to detect an ether-drift, was that most of them were performed inside opaque walls which may have dragged the ether along.

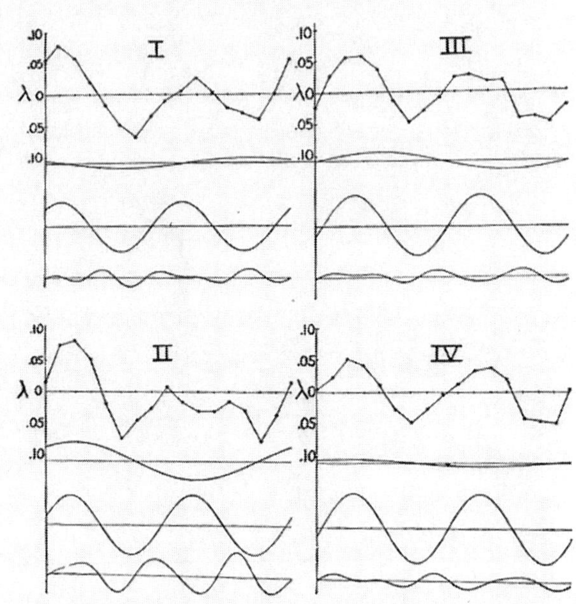


**Harmonic analysis of four data samples**

He would spend the better part of five years preparing his final report on the subject. The forty-page paper was titled, "The Ether-Drift Experiment and the Determination of the Absolute Motion of the Earth."[59] The paper included thirty-six figures. An interesting example is shown in the figure shown above. The data are from four periods in a single day. At the top of each set are plotted the raw data, and below are the results of the Henrici harmonic analysis. The upper curve is the first harmonic (almost no signal), the middle curve is the double-sine-wave where the ether-drift signal *should* be, and the bottom curve is the sum of the third, fourth, and fifth harmonics. The effect looks pretty real, the main problem being that the drift signal is still no more than ten kilometers per second. The rest of the paper gets into time-of-day and time-of-year variations and the motion of the solar system, but it does not explain the "smallness" of

59 *Reviews of Modern Physics* **5** 203-242 (1933).

the drift. The figure below shows harmonic analyzer fits to the reported drifts throughout the day and at four locations on the Earth's orbit. This was a search for systematic shifts in the drift speed as the planet spins on its axis and orbits the sun, though the results were not easily understood.

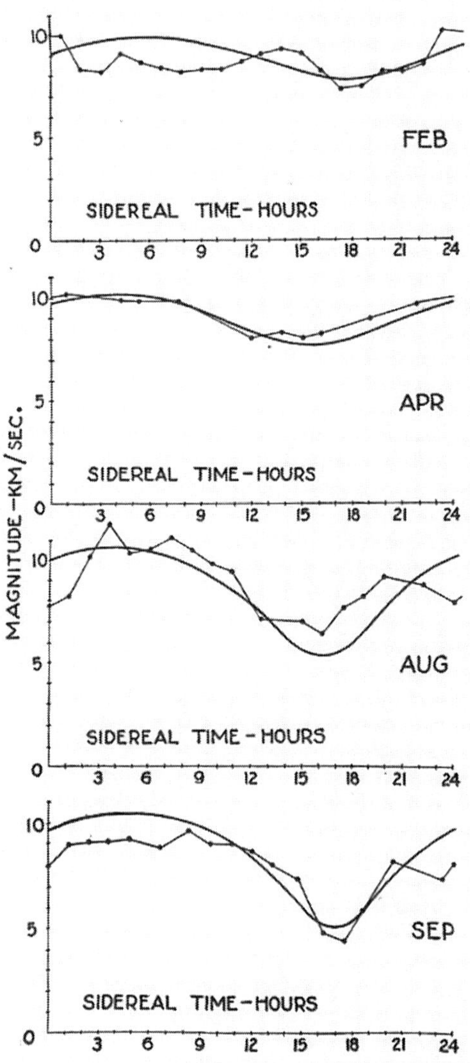


**Twenty-four-hour ether-drift results for four seasons**

Miller included brief descriptions of "other recent ether-drift experiments," for example, those of Kennedy, Picard, Michelson, and Joos, whose "drifts" were even smaller. He also reviewed "other evidences of cosmic motion," mentioning such up-to-date things as asymmetries in cosmic ray directions and Harlow Shapley's work on galactic motions.

Miller's only subsequent publication on this topic was a response to a letter from Georg Joos in a letter of his own. Joos had discussed the vulnerability of Miller's observations to temperature variations. Miller argued that such effects could not produce the *cyclical* displacements he observed. How could the interferometer arms thermally expand and contract at just the right places? The two letters appeared one-above-the-other in 1934 in the *Physical Review.* [60]

During the ten years of Miller's ether-drift work at Mount Wilson and the lengthy analyses of the data in Cleveland, astronomers around the world were pushing the limits of their art in pursuing the three other tests of relativity: gravitational deflection of starlight, gravitational redshift, and gravity's effect on Mercury's orbit. Each of these tests involved exceedingly precise measurements to detect extremely tiny effects. Contrary to the many claims made at the 1929 meeting at Cornell, in the 1930s all three tests came down on the side of general relativity.

We earlier described Eddington's famous measurements of the starlight deflection. While efforts to see the red-shifting of light escaping from the sun were not yet conclusive, studies of the spectra of an incredibly dense star, called Sirius B, led to additional support for relativity. This star, a partner in a binary system with Sirius A (the brightest star in the sky), was shown to have the mass of the sun and the diameter of the earth! With a density of 2.5 *tons* per cubic centimeter, it has an enormous gravitational field and was a splendid candidate in the search for a measurable red shift. The resulting observations agreed with Einstein's predictions. And lastly, the precession of Mercury's orbit was unambiguously shown to be consistent with general relativity.

With each of these advances, relativity prevailed, and the claim of a small ether-drift, whose size and direction were not at all understood, began to fade from the scene. Nevertheless, the gradually diminishing conservative, pro-ether faction, champions of nineteenth century Newtonian/Maxwellian physics, persisted in their battle against the progressive twentieth-century pro-relativity forces. Meanwhile, a third group, the anti-Einstein crowd, contributed their less-than-objective arguments. In his 1972 book, Loyd Swenson described these latter as "assorted crackpots, screwballs, anti-Semites, anti-Communists, and religious fundamentalists who filled out the spectrum of antirelativists."[61]

---

[60] *Physical Review* **45** 114 (1934).

[61] *The Ethereal Ether*, Loyd Swenson, University of Texas Press, 1972.

# Chapter 18 Out of the Fray

As one might expect, the 1933 Miller *Reviews of Modern Physics* paper provided ammunition for both sides of the relativity argument. Miller was sixty-seven years old; it was time to let others argue about the ether and relativity. He was eager to turn to other projects equally dear to his heart. Perhaps in the future someone might take the time to restudy his data and ferret out the source of the 10 km/sec signal. In a letter to a gentleman who had asked for information on the subject, Miller wrote: "I am sending you a reprint of the article which appeared in *Science* for June 19, 1925. This gives the history and the general conclusions. I am hardly qualified to enter into an extended discussion on the effect of the Theory of Relativity. I prefer to leave this for the mathematical physicists."

It was clear that Miller had decided to take himself out of the debate. That does not mean that he changed his mind about his ether-drift observations or about relativity. As late as 1935, Miller wrote a letter to Professor Poor reiterating his doubts about Einstein's work. Two excerpts: "I was present at the recent Pittsburgh meetings and heard Einstein's lecture. I had the opportunity of talking not only with physicists but with mathematicians and astronomers. I think there is a very general tendency to be less certain about Relativity, even to the extent of considering it rather doubtful . . . I am very much inclined to let the whole matter rest. While there are many additional experiments that I might carry out, yet I think what I have said is sufficiently definite."[62]

There were so many other duties Miller had to attend to as one of the best-known American scientists. Beginning with his public presentations on x-rays and then his books, illustrated lectures, and even radio broadcasts on musical acoustics, and finally his unsought fame in the popular press as "the

62 Letter in archives of Sheridan Libraries, The Johns Hopkins University, courtesy of Roberto Lalli.

man who proved Einstein wrong," Miller had become a nationally recognized symbol of modern science. But it went further than merely show-business. He was clearly respected by his peers, a member of the prestigious National Academy of Sciences, president of the American Physical Society, and co-founder and president of the Acoustical Society of America. All these organizations are still today at the center of the U.S. physics community.

Professor and Mrs. Miller greatly enjoyed traveling, and they made many trips around the country for lectures and conferences. Their home in Cleveland was at the center of what is called University Circle. By the 1930s, the Circle was home to the Cleveland Orchestra, a major museum of art, the two universities, and two world-class medical centers. The Millers' social life was centered about musical events, including occasions at which they would perform works for flute and piano. Between the wars, they enjoyed relaxing vacation trips to Europe, where he would prowl the second-hand shops, book stores, and galleries in search of rare flutes and related art and publications. Years later, his friend, astronomer Jason Nassau recalled, "It seems there is not an antique dealer in the world that he does not know, either by personal contact or by correspondence. Pawnshops are his specialty."

Even during the earlier Mount Wilson years, Miller had found the time to work on the second edition of his 1908 translation of the Boehm book on flutes. By the 1920s, he had accumulated much new information on Boehm and on the design and characteristics of the instrument. The "second English edition, revised and enlarged, with new biographical material and a revised list of Boehm's compositions," was published in 1922 with the support of Miller's London friends at Rudall, Carte & Co., Ltd.[63]

Miller was honored at Case by being selected as the first Ambrose Swasey Chair of Physics following the $100,000 gift from the Cleveland manufacturer of machine tools and telescopes.

Miller had many additional responsibilities as chair of a growing physics department. By 1930, he was assisted by five other professors in teaching a full array of courses for dozens of physics majors and hundreds of engineering students. Each of his five colleagues had his own research interest: Charles Hodgman on light and photography, Christian Nusbaum on magnetic properties of materials, John Albright on meteorology, Clarence Wallace on acoustics, and Robert Shankland on photon scattering. Under Miller's direction, the CSAS physics department continued to expand its academic research programs.

---

63 Paperback editions, for example from Dover Press, continue to appear to this day.

Certainly the most up-to-date, *cutting-edge*, physics research was that done by young Dr. Shankland. Shankland would bring great joy to Miller's advanced years as his major collaborator, supporter, and ultimate successor. He came from a suburb east of Cleveland to study at the Case School, earning a BS in physics under Miller in 1928. After a year and a half working at the National Bureau of Standards, Shankland returned to Case to become an instructor and to earn a master's degree, studying "The Dispersion of X-rays." Clearly, Miller's experience with x-rays thirty years earlier had something to do with the choice of that topic. Miller arranged for Shankland to spend his summers taking advanced physics courses at the University of Chicago under Nobelist Arthur H. Compton. Subsequently, Shankland spent two years in residence at Chicago, receiving his doctorate in 1935. His research was on the scattering of photons by electrons (definitely twentieth century physics), something we now call Compton scattering. He then returned to Case as assistant professor, ready to initiate a modern research program, much to the pleasure of his chairman and mentor, Professor Miller.

**Miller and his physics faculty, around 1935**
**(Shankland, second from right)**

In parallel with the expansion of Case's physics research activities, the teaching-lab facilities, especially those for advanced courses, were greatly enhanced: high vacuum equipment, precision spectrometers, high-field electromagnets, radio receivers, and transmitters. There were courses on "electron physics and x-rays," "atomic and molecular spectra," "modern physical theories." The course description of this last one reads in part: "the laws of radiation, atomic theories of matter, the periodic table, evidence for the existence of the neutron, positron, neutrino, etc." The three particles mentioned here had been only recently discovered. In striking contrast, even as late as 1938, *relativity* was not mentioned in the course descriptions.

An interesting opportunity for Miller arose in 1930, when the Cleveland Orchestra began the construction of a splendid new concert hall. A gift of philanthropist John Severance, the two-thousand-seat masterpiece was being built just across Euclid Avenue, between the equally impressive Cleveland Museum of Art and the Case and Western Reserve campuses. As a world-renowned expert on the measurement and analysis of sound, Miller was appointed acoustics consultant for the project. Especially important for the acoustical success of a concert hall is a suitable reverberation time—the time it takes for the sound to die out. As described a few chapters ago, this depends on the frequency of the sound, the volume of the hall, and the absorption by all the interior surfaces. Miller applied Wallace Sabine's techniques to the design of Severance Hall. The ideal reverberation time for a large *concert* hall is about two seconds, and for a *lecture* hall, one second or less. The gentle blending of sequential musical sounds produces a warm effect while the blending of spoken syllables is not particularly desirable.

Miller had the equipment and expertise to measure the acoustic properties of the hall, by this time using electronic microphones and recorders. Robert Shankland has written of how he and Miller set up their equipment at various places in the hall to record sounds from a variety of sources. He describes one occasion when Cleveland Orchestra conductor Nikolai Sokoloff agreed to hold high his baton at the crashing end of a symphonic piece so the scientists could record the reverberation before the audience was given leave to applaud.

When donor Severance decided to add to his generous gift, specifically for the introduction of opulent—but highly absorbent—materials and for changes in the design of the stage, Miller pointed out that the modifications would be disastrous. The reverberation time would be too short, and the sound would be trapped in the stage volume, with too little sound reaching the orchestra floor. Mr. Severance prevailed, and it would be twenty five years before some of these problems were eventually remedied, in fact, under the guidance of Miller's successor as physics department head, Shankland.

All through the 1930s, Miller continued his involvement in architectural acoustics as he participated in the design of the Chicago Opera, the auditorium of the National Academy of Sciences, several churches and chapels, including one at his alma mater, Princeton. As a founding member and second president of the Acoustical Society of America, Miller hosted a national conference of that society in the fall of 1931. The program featured papers by many of the leading American producers of acoustics-related products: General Electric, Brush, Johns-Manville, Bell Telephone, Radio Corporation of America. This meeting, held in Miller's lecture hall, provided opportunities for academic researchers to interact with their industrial counterparts.

An even more prestigious event was the fall meeting of the National Academy of Sciences, jointly hosted in 1934 by Case and Western Reserve. This was an extraordinary coup for the Cleveland institutions; the five previous meetings had been at MIT, the University of Michigan, Yale, the University of California at Berkeley, and Princeton. In Cleveland, forty-one papers were presented over the three days of the event by American leaders in all the natural sciences. The highlight was a public lecture which filled Severance Hall: "*Evolution among the Stars*" by Harvard's Harlow Shapley. It was Shapley who had discovered in 1920, in a way emulating Copernicus, that our sun is not at the center of our galaxy but rather simply an ordinary star sitting inconspicuously out on one of the Milky Way's spiral arms.

# Chapter 19 World-Class Collection

All the while that Miller was playing a rather central role in the ether drama, from the early 1920s to the mid-1930s, there was a significant parallel effort in his life—the creation of a world-class collection of flutes and flute-related material. For Miller, this quest was just as exciting and rewarding as his physics research, and it was certainly less controversial. His goal was to create a superb collection, not only of the instruments themselves but of related books, catalogs, patents, drawings, and musical scores. While the decades-long search for compelling evidence for the ether involved a continuous struggle to improve both the experimental techniques and the subsequent mathematical analyses, the creation of the flute collection moved always in one direction. He would search the world over for suitable items and purchase them if possible. His philosophy was that no object was unimportant or uninteresting, that each added something to the story. Miller sought to become one of the nation's leading *organologists*, a term applied to those who study the science of musical instruments, their classification, their history, and the technology of sound production.

If we go back to the beginning of Miller's collection of flutes, the list begins with the rosewood fife he was given when he was eleven and which his father had played during the years of the Civil War. The second entry was the piccolo Dayton played in the Baldwin College orchestra. The fourth, fifth, and sixth were the top-quality "Boehm System" instruments he bought from Rudall & Co. in London between 1896 and 1900.

Numbers eight and ten were the silver and gold flutes he built on his own in 1901 and 1905. Miller had envisioned these two projects ever since he first played the Rudall golden flute in London in 1900. Fabricating a quality instrument involved much more than drilling some holes in a hollow tube. He kept careful records of the hundreds of hours spent in creating these complex precision instruments.

Instrument number 24 must have been very special to Miller. Soon after the 1908 publication of his translation of the Boehm book, Miller received a letter from Mr. James S. Wilkins who was then living in Cuba. Wilkins explained that he had studied flute-playing with Boehm in the 1890s and that he had himself produced an unpublished English translation of Boehm's book. He was delighted with Miller's translation and his study of Boehm's flute-making techniques. In gratitude, Wilkins decided to send Miller two extraordinary items of Boehm memorabilia: the original 1847 manuscript of the book along with a flute which was built in the Boehm shop in Munich.

After this comparatively modest start, Miller would add approximately one hundred more flutes in the decade beginning in 1910, about eight hundred in the 1920s, and five hundred more in the 1930s. The timing was opportune, as many fine instruments were finding their way into the international market, including many at quite reasonable prices.

A handsome glass and silver flute, made by Claude Laurent in Paris in 1813, joined the collection in 1923 as number 378. According to Miller's meticulous records, he paid $200 (plus $3.30 S&H) to a distant heir of its first owner, President James Madison. This historic relic of French-American revolutionary camaraderie had for many years been displayed at the Smithsonian Institution.

One other record of a flute acquisition stands out. This instrument was made for a famous patron of the arts, a composer and accomplished flautist, and at the same time a powerful figure in eighteenth century Europe. This was Emperor Frederick II of Prussia, Friedrich der Grosse, or "*der alte Fritz*," depending on whether he was within earshot. Number 916 was built in Berlin by Johann Quantz around 1740. It consisted of ten different sections which could be used in various combinations to achieve the desired range. The flute, in its fine porcelain box, was passed down for one hundred forty years until it came into Miller's possession in 1930.

Professor Miller and Edith, his life-partner, occasional assistant, enthusiastic travel companion, and always supportive spouse, lived in a rented apartment on Euclid Avenue three blocks away from his office. (I am not sure how long he stayed, but the 1920 U.S. census lists Edith's father, Frank C. Easton, as living with them in the Cleveland apartment.) Even though there was generous office and laboratory space in the Rockefeller building, it soon became clear that between the physics department and their apartment, there was nowhere nearly enough space to store, much less display, the hundreds of instruments, books, catalogs, musical scores, and works of art. From the very beginning,

Miller was absolutely determined that, after his death, the entire collection should remain intact.

As early as 1924, when he was spending much of his time at Mount Wilson, Miller began a correspondence with officials at the Smithsonian Institution. By 1927, he was greatly encouraged (and Edith greatly relieved) to be informed by Dr. C. G. Abbott that the most prestigious museum in the country would not only welcome the collection in its entirety but was contemplating the construction of a superb new building to house its "fine arts" collections. Now, finally, Miller could continue to enhance the collection, knowing that its future was secure.

But the Smithsonian did not move as quickly as the Millers hoped. A year later, Dayton wrote to a colleague: "I am rather anxious to have the final disposition of the instruments determined. I would like to see them settled in Washington, and I am about ready to deposit them in the Museum. I do not see much prospect of completing arrangements with the Smithsonian until a new museum is erected." That was just not going to happen. The stock-market crash of 1929 put a quick end to such ambitious plans. The depression, on the other hand, did not put a significant dent in the continued growth of the collection which reached some twelve hundred flutes by 1934.

That year, Miller's concerns were approaching criticality. He wrote, "The collection is so large that I have no place to keep it. The instruments are all packed away in trunks, and I am seriously beginning to worry as to what will become of it. Unless I can have a little time to put it in order and arrange it for exhibition, I fear it will be destroyed or dispersed, and nothing at all will come of all the trouble I have put into it."

But that fear would soon be allayed. There were other possibilities, other museums. In June of 1934, Miller was able to report a meeting with the two key players at the Library of Congress. Herbert Putnam, sometimes described as the headstrong Librarian of Congress, had been with the LOC for thirty-five years; and the younger, more easy-going and personable Carl Engle was head of the Music Division. "They made me a definite offer to take the entire flute collection—instruments, books, music parts, etc. and to give the collection a room in the Library of Congress." Miller could only hope that they would be able to follow through on the offer, and he began to prepare a detailed inventory of all the various parts of the collection. The challenge was enormous. He described his project as "constituting five separate collections: I. Flutes and flute-like instruments. II. Books and literary material. III. Music for the flute. IV. Works of art relating to the flute. V. Portraits of flutists and composers for the flute."

In addition to the instruments, there were three thousand books, ten thousand pieces of sheet music, patents, photographs, paintings, and prints. An example of the fascinating items among the books was a rare 1680 edition of "*The Pleasant Companion: or New Lessons and Instructions for the Flagelet*." The author, Thos. Greeting, was referring in this pocket-sized manual to how easily this small flute-like instrument could "bear one company, either by land or by water."

Each piece of graphic art depicted in some fashion a person playing a flute. It was not necessarily the rarity or the value of the piece that attracted Miller's interest—just that it illustrated the popularity of the flute over the centuries. For example, the list includes an original 1496 print by Albrecht Dürer as well as a cover from the popular American magazine, *The New Yorker.* The two thousand photographs, many coming from large collections which Miller had purchased in Europe and the U.S., provide a unique record of composers and performers of the preceding fifty years. Of special interest to historians are the catalogs from instrument makers and from museum collections worldwide. Incredibly, Miller found the time and energy to prepare typewritten lists or card catalogs for everything, all of which were to accompany the collections to Washington. In addition, there were other projects on his desk, more lectures to give, trips to take, and books to write.

# Chapter 20 Passing on the Message

Building on his familiarity with the history and technology of musical instruments, as well as his expertise in the quantitative analyses of sounds, Miller decided to write a small book on the subject for the "general reader." Published by the Macmillan Company in 1935, this one-hundred-page work was titled *Anecdotal History of the Science of Sound*. It was an expanded version of a lecture he had given at the 1932 meeting of the Acoustical Society of America (ASA). Its seven chapters trace the work of at least a hundred scientists from Pythagoras in the fifth-century BC to Miller's friend, Wallace Sabine, in the twentieth AD.

In the book's preface, Miller points out how few contemporary physicists worked in acoustics. He wrote: "When the writer was in college, there were four living great men of science who were conspicuous for their work in sound, Helmholtz, Koenig, Rayleigh, and Tyndall. In the American Physical Society, before the World War, there were four members who were differentiated from their fellows by a considerable devotion to the problems of acoustics: A. G. Webster, Wallace C. Sabine, G. W. Stewart, and the author." (These four were the founders in 1928 of the ASA.) He went on to point out that most contemporary histories of science devoted only minimal space to acoustics. With the intention of rectifying that situation, he dedicated his book and its extensive bibliography to the enlightenment of the younger ASA members.

Two years later, in 1937, Macmillan published a second Miller book, once again suitable for the general reader. Miller had officially retired from teaching the year before, but it was not in his nature to waste one day. The book this time was a description of his own work in acoustics. The title was "*Sound Waves—Their Shape and Speed*," and the subtitle provides a pretty good summary of its contents: "A description of the phonodeik and its applications and a report on a series of investigations made at Sandy Hook Proving Ground."

This book was an easy one for Miller to write, as it was about his work between 1908 and 1919. In fact, it gave him the opportunity, at age seventy-one, to review and organize his many files and no doubt to reminisce a bit. Much of the material in earlier chapters of the book you are now reading derive from this review by Miller of his "phonodeik days." Although, by 1937, the electronic oscilloscope had been around for forty years, most readers must have been impressed by the simplicity and elegance of the phonodeik's "pictures of sound."

Miller's national reputation as an accomplished lecturer, and the many press reports linking his name with Einstein's, must surely have enhanced the sale of his books. In 1939, Macmillan released a third volume: "*Sparks, Lightning, Cosmic Rays: an Anecdotal History of Electricity*." It was similar in format to the science-of-sound book, but it was new territory for Miller, especially the cosmic ray sections. Miller had earlier presented three lectures on electricity as part of Philadelphia's Franklin Institute "*Lectures for Young People*." It was these lectures that he expanded into the new publication. Since the lectures had been liberally illustrated with Miller's famous demonstrations, the book would include eighty-nine images, ranging from seventeenth-century electrostatic machines to Ben Franklin's homemade generator to a van de Graaff generator at the Westinghouse high-voltage research labs. The section on cosmic rays included descriptions of radio waves; sun spots, magnetic storms and the aurora; alpha, beta, and gamma radiations; and recently invented detectors: the Geiger counter and the Wilson cloud chamber. This was a time just at the edge of the new science of "high-energy physics," when cosmic rays were providing the first glimpses of sub-nuclear particles. Robert Shankland, Miller's successor as chairman, was already doing experimental "particle physics" at Case. Miller's book showed cloud chamber pictures of cosmic rays following trajectories curved by strong magnetic fields. He explained the use of vacuum-tube electronic circuits to identify coincident counts in multiple detectors. He described the brand new cyclotron at UC Berkeley. He listed the known "elementary particles," even mentioning "barytrons" (now called mesons) and the newly hypothesized neutrino. Miller was keeping up-to-date with experimental physics.

Through all the descriptions of Miller's life and work presented thus far—his youth and education, the comet at Princeton, his marriage to Edith, the x-rays at Case, the ether search with Morley, the ingenious phonodeik, challenging relativity at Mount Wilson, his unique flute collection—we have never mentioned his personal philosophy or motivation. Perhaps that is because in his public writings and statements, Miller himself did not say very much on the subject. However, in 1936, his seventieth year, Miller gave the graduation address at Case, with the title "*The Spirit and Service of Science.*"[64]

In this address, Miller encouraged the graduates to pursue careers in science and to continue the search for an understanding of nature, or, if they chose to go into other, less selfless endeavors, like business or politics, at least to apply the honest practices of science. This appeal was followed by a few witty remarks about the scientific method. Quoting a colleague, he advised: "Think, calculate, plan, experiment, think—first, last, and all the time, *think*"; as opposed to the method commonly pursued: "Wonder, guess, putter, guess again, *theorize*." (He may have been contrasting the careful experimental work he had done on Mount Wilson with certain related theoretical proposals.) Another chuckle surely followed this remark: "An experimental result is always given with a statement of its 'probable error,' indicating its relative precision and certainty. Who ever heard of a politician concluding his speeches or of a theologian prefacing his creed with a statement as to the probable error of his opinions?"

In a more serious vein, Miller continued by listing the "realities which constitute the universe as three manifestations of absolute value: things which are eternally true: *science*; things which are intrinsically good: *ethics*; and things which are inherently beautiful: *esthetics*." In this way, he separates science from religion, although, perhaps with music in mind, he maintains a link between science and esthetics.

The last section of the commencement address dealt with "Science and Public Service." "Lest there be misunderstanding, I may state emphatically that I am not making a plea nor even suggesting that the affairs of state and society be turned over to the professional scientist. But I am proposing, indeed am demanding that the man of public affairs shall adopt the philosophy and methods of procedure which have been developed in the world of science." Later, a remark related to contemporary international politics: "The League of Nations is, when honestly considered, the most impressive application of the scientific method which the world has known and, perhaps, ever can know. How unscientific it is to consider it in a partisan spirit!" His liberal leanings (and world travel experience) begin to show.

"May we dare to hope that some of the graduates of Case School of Applied Science may be sent to the legislative branch of the government? Since men of science have exhibited an inexcusable apathy toward matters of

---

[64] Reprinted in *Science* **84** 297 (1936).

public service, it is necessary to exhort them to consecrate their abilities and knowledge to the betterment of life in general and to assume the responsibility not only for making new discoveries but also for beneficent use of these new powers, lest they be applied destructively . . . If the ideal of democracy is to be attained, I believe that the application of the true scientific spirit to the affairs of state will assist more than anything else at the present time. You are certainly of the chosen people, and I beseech you to accept the responsibility in all seriousness."

# Chapter 21 Wrapping Up

After his 1933 "final" *Reviews of Modern Physics* ether article was published, Miller essentially closed the book on the subject. There was little else that he could say about his experiments. He did not particularly enjoy being described as the man who disproved relativity. He had completed his analysis; he did not plan to repeat the experiment.

Years later, Robert Shankland described in a recorded interview a conversation with his mentor: "He gave me all his data and he said I could do two things with it, either I could burn it up or I, personally, could analyze it. He didn't want a lot of newspaper people getting a hold of it. They kept it up eternally, and every little while, there would be an article about Miller's experiment and Einstein. It was just the newspapers trying to stir up a commotion. He never quite said to me what he really thought about relativity, but his generation never was enthusiastic about it because they had grown up in a different era."

In the summer of 1938, the Millers were again in London. Miller always kept in contact with his colleagues back home. A few excerpts from a typical chatty letter to Eckstein Case:

> Dear Friend,
> It is such a pleasant sensation to get news from home! We have been here in London twelve days. There has been a "heat wave" with the "hottest day of the year"! 82°! It seems quite mild to us. I have been searching the old shops for flutes with very little success. Mrs. Miller has been shopping, moderately. We are really resting. We are both feeling better, sleeping better, and are regaining our "youth."

We shall stay here in London till August 17, when we go to Cambridge for a week, attending the British Association for the Advancement of Science. My friend, Lord Rayleigh, is the President. I found a fine old book by Francis Bacon, "*Sylva Sylvarum*," 1627, in which he describes the English flutes and gives other scientific accounts of sound.

We will probably go to the continent after the Cambridge meetings are over but have not made definite plans. We shall not go unless we both feel quite well. We hope your summer will be pleasant and restful. We both send best wishes to you and to Mrs. Case."

**Formal portrait in 1940**

By 1939, Robert Shankland, newly promoted to associate professor, had taken on many of the duties of the department chairmanship. Miller could not have been more delighted, not only because he was able to tend to his writing, his collecting, and his traveling but because the department was in good hands. In September, on a visit to New York to attend a Congress (and of course to go with Edith to another World's Fair), Miller wrote to Shankland. Some excerpts:

> "My interest in you and your work is very real and is supported by full confidence in your character, in your intelligence, and in your good judgment. No one could be better qualified to carry on work which has been the interest of my whole life. I am delighted with the present situation. Your account of the preliminary week is very satisfactory. I am sure the Department of Physics will maintain its tradition of a happy family."

Although Miller had retired from active teaching in 1936, he could not stay away from the lecture circuit. During the subsequent four years, he continued to accept invitations to speak at colleges and academic societies. His two most successful presentations were the "Spirit of Science" talk, given at both the Case and Baldwin Wallace commencements, and his "Pipes of Pan" lecture about the history and science of the flute. The Millers got to New York in February, 1940, for the winter meeting of the American Physical Society, returning once again to the Metropolitan Opera to enjoy a favorite musical experience: Wagner's *Parsifal.* Miller remained in correspondence with dozens of contacts around the world in his effort to further enhance the flute collection. In fact, he added about two dozen instruments in each of four years. In January of 1941, according to the "checklist," DCM 1426, an ivory and silver German flute was added to the collection, a gift from Dayton's sister, Mildred, of Oakland, California.

On Friday, the twenty-first of February 1941, Dayton Miller spent the afternoon working with Shankland in the Rockefeller Building. There was still a great deal to be done in preparing the materials to be shipped to Washington. That night, he suffered a fatal heart attack at home. Shankland: "He just didn't wake up the next morning, that's all."

# Epilogues

## A Most Appropriate Tribute, Miller as Teacher

Of course, there were many memorial speeches made and articles written about Dayton Miller. One of these stands out by emphasizing what was clearly one of Miller's most important contributions—bringing science to the people. This tribute was written by Miller's former undergraduate student, David Dietz. Dietz had become the Science Editor for the Scripps-Howard Newspapers. The piece appeared in the magazine, *Science*, six weeks after Miller died. It was titled "Dayton C. Miller and the Popularization of Science." [65]

Here are some selections from Dietz's article: "In company with some of the greatest figures in the history of science, he possessed the gift of making science clear to laymen and to young people . . . I saw Dr. Miller for the first time at one of his young people's lectures. The year was 1913, and I was then a junior at Central High School in Cleveland. Our scientific club, named the Faraday Club, had been invited to the Physics Laboratory of Case School of Applied Science to hear Dr. Miller lecture on sound waves. Had Professor Miller been lecturing to his colleagues in the National Academy of Sciences, he could not have made more elaborate preparations than he did for the enlightenment of our half a hundred high school boys and girls. He not only used stereopticon slides to illustrate his lecture but performed more than a dozen experiments for us upon the table at the front of the lecture room. The lecture concluded with a demonstration of the phonodeik, the device which he had invented to make sound waves visible. I still remember the delightful enthusiasm with which Dr. Miller spoke to our group of students and the enthusiasm for science which we brought away from that lecture."

---

65 *Science* **93** 319 (1941).

**Miller explains a discharge tube to three future scientists**

## Shankland, Einstein, and the Reanalysis of the Miller Data

The Second World War changed everything. The regular-degree undergraduate student population at Case dropped from about one thousand in 1942, all of them civilians, to fewer than four hundred fifty in 1944, with half of them in the military. In addition, there were hundreds of non-degree students on campus, participants in a special federal program for the rapid training of engineers and scientists.

Shankland succeeded Miller as chair of the physics department and was appointed the second Ambrose Swasey Professor of Physics. In October of 1941, Shankland published an eleven-page biography of Miller in the *American Journal of Physics*.[66]

The daunting task of getting the Miller flute collection off to the Library of Congress was completed; and in early 1942, the last crates were finally trucked off to Washington. However, because of the threat of a bombing attack on the capital, they were not delivered as addressed but rather to an underground storage location for safe keeping.

---

66 R. S. Shankland, Dayton Clarence Miller: Physics Across 50 Years. *American Journal of Physics* **9** 273-283 (1941). It is interesting that the Miller-Morley collaboration was described in only two sentences, and all Miller's subsequent ether drift research was given less than a quarter page. Shankland would later take up these topics at great length.

In mid-1942, Shankland turned the chairmanship over to his colleague, Jason Nassau. Nassau had been at Case for twenty years and was chair of astronomy and director of the Warner and Swasey Observatory. We mentioned him earlier in connection with his work with Miller in trying to untangle the connections between the ether-drift results and the motion of the solar system. Shankland left Cleveland and headed off to Columbia University to direct the Underwater Sound Reference Laboratories. As Miller's former student and successor, Shankland was an expert on the measurement and analysis of sound. The allies were in need of new technologies for the detection of enemy submarines and other ships. Shankland would be away from Case until 1946, researching underwater sound propagation and detection in New York and Florida and as the representative in London of the U.S. Office of Scientific Research and Development. After the war, he returned to Case and resumed teaching and research as chair of physics.

In 1949, Shankland wrote a four-page biographical article for the *American Journal of Physics* entitled "Albert A. Michelson at Case."[67] This was the first in a series of increasingly detailed papers on Michelson, Case's first physicist. As he looked more deeply into the significance of the 1887 Michelson-Morley experiment, Shankland wanted very much to know what role it played in the development of special relativity.[68] And what could be better in tracking this down than a visit to Professor Einstein at Princeton?

Einstein agreed to receive Shankland at his office at the Institute for Advanced Study in February of 1950. Shankland later commented that he sensed that Einstein at first expected that the purpose of the visit was to discuss the Miller results and that he seemed relieved to learn that the real reason was to discuss Michelson. At the core of the conversation was the avowal by Einstein that he became aware of the 1887 experiment through discussions with Lorentz, *after* 1905, that is, after he published the first relativity paper.

Ten months later, Shankland was back in Einstein's office. This time, Einstein seemed more relaxed and Shankland felt more at ease and brought up Miller from the beginning. He told Einstein that he and some Case colleagues were planning to search for the source of Miller's persistent signal. Einstein really got into the exchange, showing that he was genuinely familiar with the details of the Cleveland and Mount Wilson observations. He agreed that it

---

67 *American Journal of Physics* **17** 487-490 (1949).

68 There is no doubt that Shankland expected that there would be a clear causal connection between the work of Case's first physicist and the revolutionary ideas of Einstein. This claim, so often expressed in textbooks, was a source of pride for Case.

would be worthwhile to take another look. Shankland, in his later recollections, stresses Einstein's graciousness. It was likely that Einstein had little concern that relativity would be overturned but was rather simply expressing his curiosity as to what produced the apparent fringe shifts.

Einstein received Shankland twice again in 1952, once in his Princeton office, the second time at his home. Their conversations centered more on quantum mechanics than on the ether or relativity. Einstein was not very comfortable with the particle-waves, probabilities, and uncertainties espoused by Bohr and Heisenberg and Dirac. In 1950, Einstein was just about as comfortable with quantum mechanics as Miller had been with relativity twenty years earlier. As for the question of *when* Einstein learned about the Michelson-Morley experiment, Einstein this time said he was not sure and that he "just took it for granted that it was true."[69]

Since 1940, Shankland had been in possession of Miller's original data sheets from Mount Wilson. In 1952, the availability of mechanical computers might provide some advantage over Miller's simpler analytical techniques. As Shankland explained: "Well, for years I just had them locked in a closet, but then, over a period of nearly fifteen years, I would get letters from very distinguished physicists asking me what I thought about Miller's work. And during the war years in New York, physicists would ask me at lunch what I thought of it. And this all built up to a kind of a pressure. Then I thought I really should do something. So instead of burning them up, we studied them."

And so they did. Shankland was joined by three distinguished senior Case faculty members in a systematic reanalysis of the data. Fred C. Leone (1949 PhD Purdue) was on the faculty of mathematics. Gustav Kuerti (1926 D. Sci. Vienna) was an expert in aerodynamic engineering. Sidney McCuskey (1936 PhD MIT) was the head the mathematics department and professor of astronomy. The early stages of the project involved a Case physics graduate student, Robert L. Stearns, who built a mechanical computer which, it was hoped, would identify any random component in the data. In the conclusion of his Master's thesis, Stearns stated that "random statistical fluctuations in the interferometer readings can by no means account for the effect obtained by Miller." It would be necessary to seek out the origin of a non-random signal.

Shankland preserved the extensive collection of correspondence related to the development of the reanalysis paper. The text went through several very

69 Shankland provided more details of his conversations with Einstein in two later papers: *American Journal of Physics* **31** 47 (1963) and **41** 895 (1973).

different versions as the thrust of the analysis changed. Shankland invited distinguished theorists Leslie L. Foldy and Martin Klein, two of his physics department colleagues, to participate. Their arguments and suggestions resulted in significant improvements to the analysis.

By the fall of 1954, Shankland sent a draft of their paper to Einstein; and in December, he made one last trip to the great man's Princeton home. Shankland later wrote, "He began our conversation by telling me that he found our arguments convincing and a very fine paper." Einstein died the following April.

That same month, the twelve-page Case paper was published in the *Reviews of Modern Physics*, with the title "New Analysis of the Interferometer Observations of Dayton C. Miller."[70] The authors used only the Mount Wilson data since these showed the largest effect. They included data from all times of day and all seasons of the year. They first did a statistical analysis of the degree of randomness of the data, starting with the work of young Mr. Stearns. As mentioned above, this showed that the signal, small though it was, was not random. Then they went after possible temperature effects. Miller had recorded the temperature at four locations around the interferometer, at fixed times during each five hour run. First, they looked for correlations between the size of the fringe shifts and the size of the temperature gradients. Ideally, both the amplitude and the phase of the ether signal should correlate with the temperature variations. However, it would not be that clear-cut. The only conclusion that the authors could make was that the measured temperature variations were *sufficient* to cause the observed effects. They wrote: "Under the most favorable experimental circumstances, the second harmonics in the Mount Wilson data remain essentially consistent in phase and amplitude through periods of several hours and are then associated with a constant temperature pattern in the observation hut." For those in the physics community who were familiar with the results of at least a dozen technically more sophisticated repetitions of the Michelson-Morley experiment, the book on Miller's efforts was closed. But not for everyone.

## Twenty-first-Century Etherists Type I A Space for Life

For some, even today, the non-existence of the ether is unacceptable. Just as Maxwell and his contemporaries were certain that the propagation of electromagnetic waves required such a medium, there are those who, for various reasons, continue to insist on the existence of something like Maxwell's

---

[70] *Reviews of Modern Physics* **27** 167 (1955).

ether. As an example, there are those who champion a form of energy that they call orgone. This proposed phenomenon, which interacts with and affects all biological systems, is assumed to fill all of space. This energy and the related auras that surround living things are said to require the support of an ether-like medium. The unequivocal dismissal of an all-pervading ether by special relativity presents a problem for the orgone concept. Today, a search of the internet for Dayton Miller gives thousands of links associated with the ether, a similar number for acoustics and flutes and thousands more for orgone proponents and other modern antirelativists! Miller, it would seem, has become a hero in the world of these contemporary etherists. On the other hand, Shankland is sometimes described as a deceitful person who conspired with Einstein to suppress Miller's observations. Shankland did the re-analysis, it is claimed, solely to get access to Einstein and to write papers and give talks about their meetings.[71]

Some investigators have picked up where Shankland and his colleagues left off fifty years ago. They continue the search, most often, however, *not* for what may have produced a false signal but rather for solid evidence of an ether-drift. You will find images of the data sheets and pictures of Miller and his interferometer featured on many of their websites and in their publications.[72] On the other hand, some contemporary researchers have used modern computational and statistical methods to analyze Miller's eighty-five-year-old numbers.[73]

## Twenty-first-Century Etherists Type II A More Complex Space

How about other kinds of ether? The word continues to come up when "empty" space is being discussed, but it generally does not refer to Maxwell's light-carrying medium. It is not the ether Michelson and Morley and Miller

---

71 This is why the credentials of Shankland's three co-authors are mentioned above; each was a respected and established professional scientist.

72 In 2000, a leading American orgone/ether proponent visited the author at Case Western Reserve to ask about the possible existence of the original Miller data sheets. In our conversation, I took the opportunity to describe my decades-long research in experimental high energy particle physics and how every measurement was a test of special relativity. Not long after, a stack of flimsy penciled sheets was found among Shankland's papers. These were soon transferred to the Case Western Reserve University Archives where copies are available to all who ask.

73 In 2006, Thomas J. Roberts of the Illinois Institute of Technology took a look at the newly available Miller data, applying modern computational techniques. He concludes from his study that the Miller data do not support a statistically defensible fringe shift.

pursued. For example, in 1951, Nobelist Paul Dirac, one of the discoverers of quantum electrodynamics, wrote: "Aether is no longer ruled out by relativity, and good reasons can now be advanced for postulating an aether." In quantum mechanics, the uncertainty principle allows pairs of particles and their antiparticles to pop into existence out of the vacuum, momentarily violating the conservation of mass-energy, as long as they disappear very quickly. Such phenomena produce effects which have been verified experimentally. Empty space isn't empty in every sense.

Today, several CWRU research groups are participating in large multi-institutional, multinational collaborative efforts in the search for dark matter. In deep underground experiments featuring extremely sensitive instruments, professors and students are looking for such things as weakly interacting massive particles (WIMPS). Others are searching for clues to the largest component of the universe: the dark energy which is accelerating its expansion. Miller would have been fascinated to know that, almost a century after *his* efforts to understand space, his successors in Rockefeller Hall are still looking for the missing ingredients of the cosmos. Perhaps, a new, more subtle type of ether will be found.

General relativity contributes to the story as well. For example, it is expected that powerful gravitational waves are emitted when massive bodies such as black holes collide. Today's scientists are using interferometry, similar to Michelson's method, to detect contractions of space itself as these waves sweep through their billion-dollar instruments. When you add in the possibility of extra dimensions, a popular proposal today, the very definition of space is open to debate. As Miller and his contemporaries were challenged by twentieth-century relativity, today's physicists must cope with twenty-first century cosmology. The next Einstein is eagerly awaited.

## Miller's Acoustics Legacy at CWRU

Following in Miller's footsteps, Shankland spent much of his later research years studying the acoustical properties of large halls, theaters, and churches. He was central to the remodeling of Severance Hall, the home of the Cleveland Orchestra. As described above, Miller had served as acoustics consultant when Severance was built. During the 1960's, Shankland and his wife, Hilda, travelled extensively in the United States and in Europe, visiting dozens of halls and churches to measure reverberation times and other design factors which affect the quality of sound transmission.

In later years, the study of musical acoustics, initiated by Miller, continued to play a role in CWRU's physics research. In particular, there was the research on musical instruments done by Arthur H. Benade and his doctoral students in the '70s and '80s. One might even extend this lineage to William Tobocman who was a pioneer in ultra-sound medical imaging in the 1980s.[74]

## Miller's Physics Building

The Rockefeller building completed its first century of service in 2006. It continues to serve as the home of the physics department of Case Western Reserve University following the federation in 1967 of Case and WRU. The red brick exterior and the lions in the frieze under the tile roof look just as they did when its doors were opened to that first group of young scientists and engineers. The two-hundred-seat lecture hall, now decorated by a large portrait of Robert Shankland, is still home to introductory physics lectures and weekly departmental colloquia. Dayton's likeness oversees the Miller Seminar Room. A new wing on Rockefeller's southern flank was added in the 1950s, almost doubling the lab, office, and classroom space. Miller's shooting range on the fourth floor, where he photographed bullets in flight, now houses four up-to-date labs for the introductory courses while his phonodeik and interferometry research areas now accommodate a variety of research programs, which would have astounded and delighted him.

## The Dayton C. Miller Flute Collection of the Library of Congress

The appropriate way to end Miller's story, and the way which no doubt would most gratify him, is to describe the current status of his proudest achievement. His flute collection, now housed in the Library of Congress, is just as remarkable and even more important today than it was the day he wrote his will. In the year after her husband of forty-seven years passed away, Dayton's devoted wife Edith made sure that everything was prepared to go to Washington. She survived her husband by only two years.

---

[74] Miller's pioneering medical imaging research and his links with the medical profession in 1896 are recalled today by the research of CWRU's Robert W. Brown's extremely successful MRI group.

**The Library of Congress Miller Collection website**

The Miller collection is one of the world's finest examples of organology.[75] In the introduction to the library's website for the collection, Jon Newsom, chief of the library's music division, writes: "No gift has been so richly diverse in format or comprehensive in its coverage of a subject as the bequest in 1941 by Dayton C. Miller of his collection of books, prints, photographs, music, correspondence, trade catalogs, statuary, and more than seventeen hundred flutes and other wind instruments. It was Miller's vision, ahead of its time, that musical instruments, when preserved in their original condition, are invaluable historical documents."

The collection today has its own dedicated curator, Carol Lynn Ward Bamfort. It is housed in the Library's south annex in its own suite of rooms. On occasion, selected parts of the collection are put on public view in special exhibits. However, visitors are welcome and the entire collection can be seen by appointment. Among its many visitors over the years have been acousticians, world-famous musicians, and designers of musical instruments. Miller would be elated by their interest and appreciation.

Dayton Miller was a significant innovator in the application of x-rays to medical technology. For forty years, he was among the most respected American popularizers of science. He made genuine contributions to the science of acoustics. He tried his best to resolve the ether debate. His major lasting achievement can be found today at the United States Library of Congress.

---

75 *The Dayton C. Miller Flute Collection: A Checklist of the Instruments*, L. E. Gilliam and W. Lichtenwanger, Music Division, Library of Congress (1961).

# Index

**S**



**V**



**W**



**X**



**Y**

Edwards Brothers,Inc!
Thorofare, NJ 08086
22 March, 2011
BA2011081